IN YOUR FACE

IN YOUR FACE

RENO I. JOHNSON

Fresh Touch Publishing
www.arjm.org
P. O. Box 162392
Altamonte Springs Fl. 32716

Fresh Touch
——PUBLISHING——

© 2020 by Reno I. Johnson

All rights reserved solely by the author. The author guarantees all contents are original and do not infringe upon the legal rights of any other person or work. No part of this book may be reproduced in any form without the permission of the author. The views expressed in this book are not necessarily those of the publisher.

Unless otherwise indicated, Scripture quotations taken from the King James Version (KJV) – *public domain.*

Scripture quotations taken from the Amplified Bible (AMP). Copyright © 1954, 1958, 1962, 1964, 1965, 1987 by The Lockman Foundation. Used by permission. All rights reserved.

Scripture quotations taken from the Holy Bible, New International Version (NIV). Copyright © 1973, 1978, 1984, 2011 by Biblica, Inc.™. Used by permission. All rights reserved.

Scripture quotations taken from the New King James Version (NKJV). Copyright © 1982 by Thomas Nelson, Inc. Used by permission. All rights reserved.

(also the GNB) Scripture quotations taken from the Good News Translation (GNT). Copyright © 1992 American Bible Society. Used by permission. All rights reserved.

Printed in the United States of America.

ISBN-13: 978-0-98242-337-0

Contents

	Preface vii
	Introduction ix
Chapter 1	A Temporary Setback 1
	But for the Mercies of God 2
	Fragility of Human Support 5
	This Too Shall Pass 7
	Hang in There. 13
	Prayer 19
	Declarations 20
Chapter 2	I'll Be Back 21
	Delayed for Maturing 24
	Spiritual Giants Never Quit 27
	Calling Forth the Warrior Inside of You. . . . 31
	Prayer 37
	Declarations 37
Chapter 3	A U-turn 39
	A Divine Shift. 39
	God Is Turning It Around 44
	An Unlimited God 48
	Prayer 51
	Declarations. 51
Chapter 4	No More Stop Signs. 52
	Take the Brakes Off 53
	Going Beyond Human Expectations 56
	Destined for Greatness. 58
	Prayer 61
	Declarations 61

Chapter 5	Next Exit	62
	Get Rid of the Baggage	64
	Stay in Your Lane	67
	Pay Attention to the Signs	69
	Prayer	73
	Declarations	73
Chapter 6	In Your Face	74
	It Had to Have Been God	74
	Prayer	79
	Declarations	79
	Notes	81
	About the Author	83
	Contact the Author	85
	Other Books by the Author	87

Preface

THE BOOK, *In Your Face*, represents a conglomerate of biblical research, personal experiences, and the stories of others as it relates to the awesomeness of God as manifested in and through His children. The words on these pages come alive when reading. It is an easy read, as the writing is about issues with which we all can identify. The stories are so powerful and the promises of God so clear that the book is appropriate for a variety of age groups, including teenagers. The material owes its existence to the inspiration of the Holy Spirit, many hours of reading and rereading the Bible, and many conversations and collaborations with Christian friends, teachers, and small group discussions.

The inspiration for writing In Your Face came from the Holy Spirit, and I give all glory to God for this accomplishment. I also wish to thank my wife, Shandaly, and my two lovely daughters, Ranaé and Reishonda Johnson, for their love and support.

Introduction

In Your Face is designed from the beginning to the end to encourage and motivate the readers to go beyond the norm of the average believer and to experience the all-powerful, all-wise, and majestic God. Throughout the book there are constant reminders that good will prevail against evil and that once we surrender to the will of God, we are destined for success. The very name of the book evokes a feeling of victory for the reader, as it claims a celebration for the children of God right in the face of the enemy. The central theme is that our lives are undergirded with purpose and, as such, God will direct us in paths which at times are uncomfortable and unfamiliar; but know for sure that these same paths will lead to the ultimate actualization.

While our current disposition can have some effect on the future, it does not determine our final outcome. However, many people confuse the current rejections and frustrations with the future plans of God. Despite humanity's limitations on our future, God will take us beyond human imaginations. There is a mysterious element in life that allows persons of low esteem to rise above the precepts and expectations of the prophets of doom.

Over the years this mysterious selection and promotion by the Divine has caused many to be left bewildered, pondering how could this be so? Some of the most influential people in the world would testify that they came from very humble beginnings; perhaps many were counted as least likely to succeed for economic, social, or spiritual reasons. One of the greatest American presidents, Abraham Lincoln, has a history that, when told, makes people wonder how someone with so many challenges could ever become president. Oprah Winfrey, one of the wealthiest African Americans, wrote a book which outlines her childhood struggles with abuse. Paula White, one of America's most popular televangelists, testifies of how she was on welfare, living on the streets. Our very own Dr. Myles Munroe, an internationally renowned teacher and bestselling author, came from the backseat of a small church to the world's stadium. The list of examples can go on and on, for there are countless men and women who came from humble beginnings. In this book you will discover how God takes delight in preparing a table before you in the face (presence) of your enemies.

As you continue to read this book, you will discover the many ways God takes the rejects of society—those disdained, scorned, and overlooked by others—and makes them shine like the noonday sun in the face of the enemy. In the sentiments of Daniel, we make our plans but it is God that commands. (See Daniel 2:20–21; 4:17.) *In your face!*

Chapter 1

A Temporary Setback

THE ENEMY WOULD have us to believe that the problems or adverse situations we might have found ourselves in yesterday (or today) can prevent us from operating in tomorrow's blessings. Rather, God has equipped us in such a way that these temporary dispositions serve merely to mature us to function in a godly manner once we embrace the rich promises of God. According to *The Free Dictionary*, setback is defined as "an unanticipated or sudden check in progress; a change from better to worse."[1] Throughout life we are faced with various unplanned events that can either break us or make us. Our response to such unforeseen events will determine the difference between success and failure. Like Tommy Lasorda said, "The difference between the impossible and the possible lies in a person's determination."[2] You must be determined to press through whatever you run into.

God has placed within us the ability to survive whatever obstacles come in our pathway; we just need to obey His instructions. As stated in Romans 8:28, "And we know that in all things God works for the good of those who love him, who have been called according to his purpose" (NIV). In most cases if it had not been for divine delay we would have been like a hot-headed teenager who upon receiving the keys to his/her first car gets into an accident. When scolded by the father for reckless driving exclaims, "No big deal; it's only a car." Thus, the temporary setback allows us the time to reflect and learn to appreciate the reprimands and/or gifts given by our heavenly Father.

But for the Mercies of God

God takes delight in spreading a table before us in the presence of our enemies, not because of our worthiness but for His glory. The psalmist said in chapter 37: "Fret not thyself because of evildoers, neither be thou envious...Delight thyself also in the LORD: and he shall give thee the desires of thine heart" (Ps. 37:1, 4). All this needless worrying about the seemingly prosperity of the enemy and fretting about the threat they pose to us is useless. Instead of giving so much attention to our enemies, God desires that we delight ourselves in Him.

Have you ever stopped to listen to the testimonies and prayers of some folks? More times than necessary Christians glorify the problems. Their prayers are usually a retelling of the problem, and even the testimonies recite the hidden anger for the evildoers as opposed to praising God for His provisions. Too often Christians are too busy chasing after the devil to recognize or acknowledge the blessings of God. Yes, the enemy is real; but God is using the enemy to throw you a banquet.

Just because God has made us the honored guests in the presence of the enemy doesn't give us the authority to become haughty or lord over others. The favor of God upon our lives is an unmerited (undeserved) gift. We must use it for His glory. Moreover, the table that God is about to spread is one that should move us to live out the passage of scripture that says, "If your enemy is hungry, feed him; If he is thirsty, give him a drink" (Rom. 12:20, NKJV). Most of us can rejoice at the thought of being at the head table, but it is hard to go beyond this point to allow our bowels of mercy to reach the onlookers (in this case the enemy).

God's mercy is not merely to be placed on a shelf to gather dust; it is to be shared with others.

Despite the Christian's spiritual endeavors, there is not one person who can boast of deserving God's mercy. We are reminded that "all our righteousness is as filthy rags" (Isa. 64:6). It is but for the mercy of God and not any goodness of our own. We read in John 8:1–11 about the woman who was caught in the act of adultery. The entire town gathered with stones to slay her. However, Jesus made one statement that silenced the entire crowd; He said, "He that is without sin among you, let him first cast a stone at her" (v. 7). One by one they left until she stood alone. People can be quick to point out the shortcomings of others while overlooking their own faults. If you were to allow the accusations or past mistakes to keep you from pursuing the kingdom, you would end your life without achieving your God-given purpose. What I admired most about this story is that though they brought her to Jesus so that He might sanction their actions, instead of sentencing her to death, as was the custom in that day, Jesus set her free and forced the crowd to search themselves. God's ways are not like men's, so stop allowing people to dictate to you. *But for the mercies of God!*

A popular misconception is that we can buy the favor of God or work our way into righteousness. God does not need our money; remember, He spoke and the heavens and the earth came into being. Moreover, as the children love to sing at Sunday school, God has the whole world in His hands. It is amazing how many persons abuse the sacredness of giving a tithe or offering. It is often said by the carefree church goers, "I sent my tithes and offering so God has to bless me!" While God will keep His word to give bread to the sower, God requires more than just a tithe or offering. God wants relationship (*koinonia*); that's why He admonishes us to delight ourselves in Him. To "delight" indicates some sort of pleasurable moment, nothing forced or contingent upon anything else. It is like panting after God as a deer pants for the water brooks (Ps. 42:1). Once our hearts long for God and we seek to keep His commandments, there is a transferring of favor on our lives. However, there is not one who can demand the favor of God to rest upon them; but for the mercies of God we are not consumed but favored (Lam. 3:22; Eph. 2:4).

It puzzles me when I study the biblical accounts of the Israelites. These were folks who had seen God do wonders like part the Red Sea, defeat the Egyptians, drop manna from heaven, and so forth; yet they forsook the true and living God to follow gods made of wood or crafted by the hand of men. The Israelites were wayward (rebellious) serving God during the hard times and forsaking Him to serve pagan gods during times of prosperity. At first the people were faithful to the Lord, but they gradually fell into idolatry. Then God punished them by allowing their enemies to enslave them, until they repented and called upon Him to rescue them.

God would then raise up leaders called judges to defeat the enemy. Hence, the Book of Judges is an excellent study of the mercies of God. Although the author of the Book of Judges appears to be anonymous, some documents (including Jewish tradition) indicate that Samuel or one of his students may have written this book.

As long as the children of Israel were obedient to the commandments of God, they were protected from their enemies; but once they began to serve other gods, the protection of God would then be removed leaving them accessible to their enemies. There were times when the sins of Israel became so great that the stench of it reached God's nostrils. However, God never left them completely; He always delivered them from the oppression. Often those whom God choose were not popular or met the status quo; however, it was evident that it only could have been the hands of God.

The psalmist is correct when he declared that God is merciful and slow to anger (Ps. 103:8; 145:8), for indeed the best of us have fallen inexcusably but God still raised us to higher heights. A temporary setback! While going along on this journey called life, the temptations often overtake us; and as a result many are prone to wander and leave the God they love. In many respects we are no different from the Israelites, the chosen of God, who were continuously chasing after gods that could not help them while forsaking the great I Am (Exod. 3:14). Yet, there is something that draws us back to God and whispers to our fainting heart to stay with God. In His infinite mercy God comes searching after us, raising up great warriors to rescue us from the grasp of the enemy and demonstrating His power in phenomenal ways.

Fragility of Human Support

Perhaps you are one of those persons who have made yourself available for God to work in and through. Unlike your counterparts you refuse to worship other gods or to lower your standard of holiness. Or maybe you find joy in being in the presence of God as opposed to dwelling in the counsel of the ungodly. Hence, God has chosen to display His glory through you, but the people around you are refusing to support you. Don't be discouraged if you are abandoned or surrounded by those who are trying to sabotage your future. Remember, people are not always going to support you; there will be times when you have to encourage yourself on this journey. Nevertheless, what is important is that you keep your relationship with God strong.

The power to promote you is in the hands of God, thus humanity has no say in your success. You might be saying, "Who am I that God would favor me?" In the Book of Judges, most of the persons chosen by God were poor, unpopular, and unqualified by men's standards; yet they simply made themselves available to carry out God's assignment. Jephthah, one of the judges mentioned in the Old Testament, for instance, became known as a mighty man of valor but he was the son of a harlot. Judges 11:1 says, "Now Jephthah the Gileadite was a mighty man of valour, and he was the son of an harlot." I assume that while growing up in Gilead, many persons jeered at him and despised him because of his mother's reputation. Perhaps at school or in the community few people addressed him by his actual name; instead they would probably say, "There goes the harlot's son!" But little did they know God had a plan for the harlot's son. *Human support is fragile!*

The attacks will come from those you least expect once God begins to demonstrate His handiwork through you; case in point, God hand-picked Jephthah for greatness. This appointment was not accepted by his own relatives; they refused to have him as their leader. Like Jephthah, many are facing this same kind of rejection. Prior to promotion of any kind (be it spiritual or temporal), your relatives or so-called friends embraced you with opened arms; but since the increase there is a noticeable shift in their attitudes. In general, rejection hurts; but when it is inflicted by your own people, it cuts straight through the heart. The good thing, however, is that once God sets His stamp of approval upon you, it does not matter who disapproves. It is God who raises up and pulls down leaders. It is unnecessary to worry about those who are not willing to support you; just stay in the will of God and get ready to experience divine reversal. David declares in Psalm 23:5, "Thou preparest a table before me in the presence of mine enemies." There must be enemies in order to experience the table. God is going to do for you what He has predetermined right in your enemies' face.

Jephthah was created by God with all the qualities and abilities that he would ever need. John C. Maxwell once said, "A leader is one who knows the way, goes the way, and shows the way."³ Jephthah was not a wimp or a "fly by night" but a man of valor, a true leader. In a military sense, he was a skilled warrior. You may have experienced or are currently experiencing what Jephthah felt when he was mishandled and mistreated by his own folks. Whether in your home, on your job, or even in the church, you are experiencing hardship. Do not give into the enemies devices; you are being prepared so that you can be positioned and God will finish what He has started in your life (Phil. 1:6). I love what William Shedd said; and I quote, "A ship in the harbor is safe, but that is not what ships are built for."⁴ My friend, you are God's battle ship and you can no longer hang around the harbor (mediocrity) because you were built for the ocean (greatness); so start sailing. Wow, you ought to just shout and let the enemy know that you have left the harbor! Remember, human support is fragile! Prepare yourself; because the minute they speculate that you have the ability and the qualities to supersede them, the attacks will come from the left, right, and center. You may find yourself on the run, like in the case of David as he fled from Saul; but remember that God is a present help in the time of trouble (Ps. 46:1). Get ready for greatness!

THIS TOO SHALL PASS

New Testament narrative in Mark chapter 4, where Jesus calms the raging sea (vv. 35–41), serve to remind those whose faith is anchored in Christ that storms will come but they are certain to pass away—a temporary setback! Too often the uncomfortable feelings that come from the thumping waves and imbalanced experiences that stem from blowing winds make us lose sight of the fact that Jesus is still on board. The disciples, like we often find ourselves, had just witnessed the miraculous power of God and heard His awesome teaching, yet they found themselves in disarray. Firstly, they were startled by a swift shift. The story unfolds with Jesus and His disciples enjoying a beautiful boat ride en route to the other side. However, a familiar sea route frequented by many developed into a nightmare for the disciples; they were caught in a fierce storm and became fearful for their lives. Don't be caught unaware; change is inevitable. Yet God is constant as often quoted, God is "the same yesterday, and to day and for ever" (Heb. 13:8).

The winds of life might blow, but you just hang in there. This too shall pass! I could imagine these experienced boatmen fighting with everything in them to keep the boat afloat and gradually becoming weary. The second lesson here is that while experience and knowledge is good, there are some situations we will find ourselves in that only God can get us out of. These men, especially Peter and the sons of Zebedee, were skilled fishermen and experts in boating; yet this storm forced them to seek advice from a greater source. One of the reasons why we stay in bondage so long and undergo lengthy hardship is due to pride that prevents us from admitting that we do not have all the answers. Many of the problems we face can be resolved quickly if we decide not to lean to our own understanding, rather in all our ways to acknowledge God so that He can direct our path (Prov. 3:5–6).

We were not given any time frame as to how long the men battled the stormy seas; but we know that they eventually came to a place of hopelessness, even as Jephthah did, and sought refuge in God. This too shall pass! Often it is said that unless an addict hits rock bottom there is no genuine desire for recovery. While this is not true of all cases, there is some truth in this statement for Christian practices.

For example, some of our best prayers were uttered on knees of despair. We commune more intimately with God when we are in trouble and in need of His favor. Seldom do we launch into God's presence when we are happy and enjoying the fat of the land. God desires us to love on Him equally in the good times and the bad, for our continuity is wrapped up in Him.

Frustrated and tired of the challenges, the disciples shouted, "Master, carest thou not that we perish?" (Mark 4:38). How often we encounter folks who, when faced with trials or problems, jump to the conclusion that God must not care? God cares, but you must be processed (go through the fire) because He's not investing in anyone who has not been processed for the promise. Jephthah was called but also had to be processed before receiving the position God had predestined for him.

Many years ago I listened, almost to tears, as a preacher shared with the congregation his testimony of his father's death. It was no ordinary testimony, as it was filled with pain. The preacher said, "I was so mad with God when my father died, I stopped coming to church; I felt like God had failed me." He went on to say, "I had asked God to heal my father; but instead my father died, then I wondered how God could do something like this? I prayed and prayed, and yet he died." Wow, what a testimony and what misguided perception of God! Like a spoiled child who is used to his father meeting his every demand, this preacher threw a tantrum at God. Like the disciple, this preacher was crying, "Jesus, if You cared then You would do something!"

Some of you are now in the fire, being processed to go higher, and are crying, "God, if You cared You would get me out of this." God cares, cares that you go to the next level. Nevertheless, we can't measure how much a person cares by the level of control we have over them or by our ability to make them our puppets. Like a good father, God cares enough to give us what is best for us and loves us enough to deny us our selfish wants. Like Jephthah was processed and had to experience his storm, so do you. But remember, *this too shall pass!*

By now you might be wondering what happened to the preacher. He matured and realized that God is in control. While it was his desire that God grant his father a physical healing, God actually healed his father spiritually. When the mourning had subsided and the preacher looked back over his father's habits, he concluded that if God had not taken him suddenly his father would have gone back to some of his uncontrollable habits. In other words, he realized that God's ways and plans are perfect. Friends, what often seems like final destruction is simply an avenue for God to be exalted in our lives and for us to journey safely to what He has promised. Dottie Rambo puts it this way in her song, "Sheltered in the Arms of God:"

> So let the storms rage high, the dark clouds rise,
> They won't worry me, for I'm sheltered safe within
>   the arms of God;
> He walks with me and naught of Earth can harm me,
> Sheltered safe within the arms of God.

God is in control and what you are experiencing will not kill you but rather build you. As Ralph Waldo Emerson said, "Big jobs usually go to the men who prove their ability to outgrow small ones."[5]

When our anchor is in Jesus Christ, we can relax. The disciples panicked because they forgot who was on board. Their eyes were centered on the winds and waves and not on the Christ. It is so easy to let our circumstances and the events around us to cause us to lose focus. Remember, while on your way to the other side (the place of promise) you will encounter some storms; but keep in mind that He that sent you is with you and certainly won't leave you now, because He has a word to fulfill. Jephthah had to remain focused even in his storm. If you are an employer or supervisor, a disorderly employee can make the work environment perturbed (troubled, disturbed). For a pastor disgruntled leaders can make the church atmosphere uninviting. Even at home the air can be cold and uncalculated (uncertain) because of a grumbling spouse. We can all attest to being in certain conditions that really tested our faith because of what we saw happening around us. When the winds and the waves are raging and the storm clouds are rising, we must trust in the captain of our soul, the Alpha and Omega, the God who finishes whatever He starts. The apostle Paul said it this way in Philippians 1:6, "Being confident of this very thing, that he which hath begun a good work in you will perform it until the day of Jesus Christ." *This too shall pass!*

Many readers are surprised to find Jesus in the bow asleep. This doesn't amaze me. Relax; He's God, He knows where He's taking you and just what you will pass through to get there. Over the years, I have reminded myself of how this awesome God slept through the storm and have used this as a pillar of strength to get through boat rides. Once the instructions for traveling are given and the captain pulls away from the dock, I rest my head in a comfortable position and I am off to sleep. Some folks claim they need to stay awake to keep watch. Why keep watch? That's the job of the captain (God) and the crew (the angelic host). I've concluded that some folks love to remain awake so that they can keep a record of how many times the boat tossed and how many waves hit the bow. It is really to worry and engage in panic exercises that some remain awake. Worrying is not the answer to get through a storm. As instructed in severe (ruthless, rigorous) weather, we are to remain calm so that we can take the appropriate action for survival. Stay calm, my friend; God is at the helm, you're on your way to greatness and the table is about to be spread in the face of your enemies.

What are the storms in your life? How are you dealing with them? The disciples came to a point where they had to seek the help of Jesus. They awoke Him and appealed to His compassion: "Don't You care about us?" Jesus was disappointed that they did not know the level of His love for them and that they had no faith. Friends, without faith it is impossible to please God (Heb. 11:6). It takes exercising our faith to move the hands of God. The Bible said: "Abraham believed God, and it was counted unto him for righteousness" (Rom. 4:3). All God requires of you is to believe what He has promised He is able to perform.

Jesus spoke and immediately things began to change; the winds and the waves were at peace. What makes you think that your storms are too difficult for Jesus to calm? Why do you walk around with your head hung down as if your situation is irreversible? Jesus Christ has authority over the winds and the waves, and He can change your situation in an instant. The disciples had to move from self-reliance to complete dependence on Jesus. While this showed lack of faith, it also implies that Jesus will answer us when we cry out for His help and there is no time constraint on how quickly He will resolve the matter. As we see in this story, the winds and waves came to an abrupt end at the command of Jesus: "Peace, be still" (Mark 4:39). Booker T. Washington once said, "Success is to be measured not so much by the position that one has reached in life as by the obstacles which have been overcome while trying to succeed."[6] This too shall pass (whatever you're going through)!

Hang in There

Visible signs of the favor of God are evident in everything you do; in fact, your very presence attests to the power of God. We read in Judges 11 about Jephthah, a mighty deliverer who was sent by God to rescue the people of Israel. Jephthah had the innate (inborn) qualities to lead this people. Everything that he needed to function as the head of this nation, he was given by God from the foundation of the world. No doubt there were times when Jephthah felt inadequate and perhaps questioned his purpose for living. On the other hand, there were times when he felt sure that there was something greater out there for him to do. Like many, Jephthah struggled with his calling, although the signs of God's hand upon him were evident.

In a small village surrounded by misfits and outcast, certainly Jephthah was tempted to believe that his very existence was a random occurrence. The grim and gloomy episodes in that village perhaps left little room for creative thinking and futuristic planning. In the eyes of the masses, he was what some would term "a product of his environment," and as such doomed for menial (basic) achievement, if any at all. But in God's repertoire (catalog) Jephthah was created to be an agent of change and make his mark in the chronicles of history. Like Jephthah you are God's agent of change and that's why you are being attacked from within and without; but you must hang in there, the best is yet to come!

Hang in there despite the struggles; God has a plan. God is working behind the scenes to bring His purpose to the conclusion He has foreordained. Stop sneaking in through the back door or hiding in the corner. In other words, stop hiding your abilities; you are great and the folks around you know it. Jephthah's brothers knew when they saw him that he was not ordinary, so they wanted to get rid of him. The fate of many resides in your actions. God is depending on you; He has anointed you with a turnaround anointing and wherever you show up things have to change.

The people around you already know that you are not ordinary, and it's about time that you begin to realize it yourself. Many are failing because they have lost that push, press, and pursue that they once had. The apostle Paul declared in Galatians 6:9, "Let us not become weary in doing good, for at the proper time we will reap a harvest if we do not give up" (NIV). Hang in there; you've come too far to miss the end results of your pain. Roger Bannister said, "The man who can drive himself further once the effort gets painful is the man who will win."[7] The results on your job, in the church, at school, at home, and in your neighborhood would be different if you were to walk in the authority that God has entrusted to you.

We, as children of God, are His ambassadors here on earth; therefore, it is incumbent upon us to carry out God's biddings. What you are experiencing right now is only a temporary setback; remember, God has a plan and after you would have been buried by your haters you will rise up in power. Hang in there, because you are about to experience a *silent explosion*. In other words, your enemies are not going to hear when the favor of God explodes in your life, but they will see! *In your face!*

Yes, when you take your rightful place and exercise the authority given to you as joint heirs with Christ, you will be persecuted. They said all manner of evil about Jesus who went about doing good (Matt. 9:35); so what more will they do to us? You must hang in there. The Bible reminds us that the world hates that which is not its own (John 15:18-19). We do not belong to the world; we belong to God, so we cannot expect the world to endorse our aspirations and/or achievements.

Many folks are avoiding you because they suspect that God is about to do something supernatural in your life. Like

Jephthah's brothers, they can see and sense the hand of God and His favor upon you; and they're not happy, because it's you. Folks will do and say all manner of evil to frustrate you so as to prevent you from operating in what God has ordained for you. Well, they might as well eat their hearts out because it's going to happen, you're about to be favored with force. What is favor with force? It is favor that cannot be controlled, and it's about to take you over, right in their face. My friend, they are not worth your hate. Therefore, it is vital that you stay grounded and stand firm, refusing to give in or to give up. It's just a temporary setback for a permanent come back. *Hang in there!*

To believe in one's self is a priceless commodity. People with high self-esteem are not easily distracted or discouraged. High self-esteem is not the same as a proud or high-minded individual; high self-esteem is simply someone who believes in themselves despite what others might think or say. We must always be careful not to become puffed up or haughty as the Bible tells us that pride goes before a fall (Prov. 16:18). Rather, as the apostle Paul puts it in Romans 8:35–39, we must be so persuaded that nothing would be able to separate us from the love of God. In addition, nothing would be able to cause us to abandon the promises of God. We should be so persuaded that God's promises are yes and amen (2 Cor. 1:20)!

When our hearts are locked into God's mandate, then we are sure to excel. For some of you the big question is how can these things be since your capabilities or resources do not meet the requirements? Maybe you can't see a way out of poverty or generational curses; or perhaps people have been prophesying doom over you since childhood. Don't let this discourage you; when God's time comes, you're coming out. People will judge you based on their limited insight, but this does not determine who you are or what you are capable of doing. God has the final say; and when God speaks everything must line up. My comrades, just take God at His word and do not let man's limitations determine your achievement. Moreover, the qualities that you need are already on the inside of you. However, if you allow the people in your environment to discourage you, you will miss out on your blessings. *Hang in there!*

Whenever God anoints you, whenever He elevates you, whenever He blesses you, whenever He gives you the new house, car, and so forth, He is going to do it right in the face of those that said it could not happen. Jephthah's brothers said to him in Judges 11:2b, "Thou shalt not inherit in our father's house; for thou art the son of a strange woman." That's what they were saying, but that's not what God said and whatever God said shall prevail. I don't want my blessings to be handed to me in my backyard or through some dark alley; I want my blessings released to me right in the face of my enemies. Then those who once despised me, who were certain that nothing good would happen for me, will know that God is in control.

It is so difficult to stare the enemy in the eye from day to day with a smile and a pure heart. Remember, the enemy is like the persons sitting in a football stadium cheering for the opposite team hoping for your defeat. But when God's time comes, He will allow an interception; and when you make the touchdown, even the most adamant spectators will stand with priceless expressions of awe on their faces. All I can say right about now is, "Wow! Wow! Wow! God is awesome!" Here's what the Bible says in Job 5:12: "He frustrates the devices of the crafty, so that their hands cannot perform their enterprise or anything of [lasting] worth" (AMP).

Here's the revelation: God at times will allow our enemies to run with that which is not theirs but belongs to us from the foundation of the world; but just when they think they are going to score a touchdown and all of their fans are cheering them on, He hits them a knockout blow causing them to fumble the ball releasing it into the air only to be intercepted by us. And by the time they recover, we are in the end zone dancing and praising God! And guess what? The game is over and we have won! My friend, you should give God a shout right about now; and you should stop trying to convert your enemies, for they have a purpose which will serve to enhance the joy and fulfillment you will gain when God brings you out of the wilderness into your season of the overflow. *Hang in there!*

The Bible tells us that God uses the simple things to confound the wise (1 Cor. 1:27). Jephthah, for example, was certainly a capable soldier, but his social position was not up to man's standards. He was the son of a harlot, he did not have the right background, and according to his brothers he was not qualified for the inheritance and surely was not able to lead them. However, in God's view Jephthah was the perfect man for the job. Friends, man plans but God commands; and we must not allow their plans and boundaries to cause us to pull back on God. We must not allow what they (the haters) think and say to dictate how much faith we will exert into God's plans. Hang in there; and I guarantee you that when the dust is settled, you will come out on top. *In your face!*

Several times before being ordained an apostle or even recognized as a pastor (just a mere minister in my previous church), I have been invited to speak at pastoral anniversaries and major conferences. In my heart I questioned God if I was worthy or even qualified to speak at such events and to persons of such great significance in the religious arena. It would seem more appropriate to have someone of equal status or even greater to speak at such events. Yet God allowed the invitation to be extended to me, a "no name" preacher. Once I got over this odd occurrence and approached the task with confidence that it is God who will speak through me, I soon realized that qualifications are relative (family) to God. Our natural certification is a great asset, but it is not the ultimate source of promotion. Every time I had to speak at an event, God played me like an instrument and the reviews were all favorable with subsequent invitations to speak at future events. *Hang in there because God will fulfill His will!*

Often people feel they can determine the mind of God and claim they speak on behalf of God when they make a requirement for such standards. However, the Bible declares that God's thoughts are not like our thoughts, neither our ways like His ways (Isa. 55:8). God sees beyond your shortcomings, and He knows your potentials. God has placed a special gift in each of us, and He knows how to bring it out and exactly what it takes to polish us.

The illustration of a crumbled hundred dollar bill remains as significant to me as the first time I heard it. A hundred dollar bill does not lose its value because someone crushed it, stamped on it, or even spilled something on it. As long as the serial number is visible and it is legible, a hundred dollar bill still has the same value as when it first came off the press. The same illustration can be applied to us: after being attacked, crushed, mistreated, abused, and rejected, our DNA still will prove that we are royal priesthood, anointed and appointed by God.

God has given you the ability, power, gifting, and anointing to carry out your assignment. And oftentimes those who are not in tune with God will believe that they're not capable of handling the task. But what they fail to realize is that who God calls He qualifies and who He qualifies He anoints and who He anoints He appoints. My comrade, be assured that once God is through processing you,

you will be more than able to accomplish the tasks with exceptional and noteworthy finesse. Men may overlook the gifting, talents, and the anointing that God has entrusted within you; but you need to stay in tune with God so that He can direct you and you need to totally follow the path that leads to wholeness. In addition, we need to let the voice of God overpower that of humanity. Hence, when God says we can do all things through Christ who strengthens us (Phil. 4:13), we must hear this above the sounds of doom and failure.

The apostle Paul asked this question in 1 Corinthians 2:16: "Who hath known the mind of the Lord, that he may instruct him?" The ones we least expect are those God is looking for; like the prostitutes, murderers, robbers, etc. Once converted, God will make them shine like the noonday sun. God is looking for men and women who, after He has anointed, will not attribute their success to self but will give Him (God) all the glory. Don't be discouraged, God will bring you into a fertile land and He will make you to know joy and contentment. Someone once said that hardship is only a test; in order to get to your blessing, you must first pass the test. Remember, no pain no gain. *Hang in there!* What you are going through is just a temporary setback. The best is yet to come!

PRAYER

> *Loving God, in the perfect name of Jesus Christ I ask You to remove every spirit of discouragement and depression from my heart due to the temporary setbacks in my life. Let me receive inspiration from Your Word, which declares do not grow weary in well doing for in due season I will reap if I do not lose heart (Gal. 6:9, NKJV). I pray that I will be anxious for nothing (Phil. 4:6, NKJV) and*

that my soul will find rest in you; my deliverance comes from you in the time when my soul asked, "How long will you assault me?" (Ps. 62:1, 3, NIV). *Lord, help me to be confident of this very thing that He who has begun a good work in me will complete it until the day of Jesus Christ* (Phil. 1:6, NKJV). *Amen.*

Declarations

I decree and declare that there will be no more setbacks in my life, in Jesus' name!

I decree and declare that the fragility of humanity will not discourage me but rather cause me to focus on God's faithfulness, in Jesus' name!

I decree and declare that by the mercies of God I will survive and become great, in Jesus' name!

I decree and declare that this too shall pass—the trials, the disappointments, and the setbacks—so that I can come into my "wow" season, in Jesus' name!

I decree and declare that I will hang in there until God brings everything to pass that He has promised me, in Jesus' name!

Chapter 2

I'll Be Back

Life can throw us some serious blows, leaving wounds that appear to be incurable. A good friend of mine by the name of Dave was hit with several of those terrible blows, as he underwent a never ending cycle of struggles. Many onlookers were confused by this since him and his wife were devoted Christians and both faithfully served as leaders in the church. Nevertheless, within two weeks fire devoured Dave's life-long investments. That is, Dave, a fisherman by trade, jumped from his exploding vessel into the sea and swam in the distance to watch his livelihood (his fishing boat) go up in flames. He rejoiced that he had escaped without injury, but he was completely clueless about future employment. It seemed as if this was going to be the most difficult financial situation he had to endure. Dave realized that he had to depend upon God, as he had been doing in the past. He kept his faith grounded in God's ability to make ways out of no way, trusting that God will bring him back to the top.

Waiting on God when life's circumstances escalates require us to go beyond normal faith talk; it calls for true endurance. The following week, Dave's wife was outside hanging out clothes when she realized her baby was alone in the house. She rushed inside, retrieved the babe, and came back out to continue her chores. Within minutes the house was ablaze with fire. Here is what Dave exclaimed, "Thank God my family was not in the house!" In other words, Dave said, "I am going to praise God anyhow." And that's the mind set we must develop during the process (the refiners fire).

Here's what God told the Israelites in Jeremiah 29:

> For thus says the Lord, When seventy years are completed for Babylon, I will visit you and keep my good promise to you, causing you to return to this place. For I know the thoughts and plans that I have for you, says the Lord, thoughts and plans for welfare and peace and not for evil, to give you hope in your final outcome.
> —JEREMIAH 29:10–11, AMP

God told His chosen people, "You're going to experience hardship and lose some stuff for about seventy years. And no matter what you do, it's going to happen. But when the appointed time (*kairos*) comes, I am going to visit you and perform My good word toward you." You may have lost everything and been damaged, scorned, rejected, abused, mistreated, and misused; but know for certain that God has a plan for your life and after your wilderness experience, the greater is coming.

Like Jephthah, some of us have lost everything and have been thrust out of the place and from among the people among whom God has ordained for us to shine in their midst; but remember that God has a plan. Jephthah had to flee from his father's house to dwell in the land of Tob. Judges 11:3 states, "Then Jephthah fled from his brethren, and dwelt in the land of Tob." Tob was a desolate region filled with worthlessness and worthless people. But for Jephthah, it was an excellent place for kingdom preparation. On his way out, I believe Jephthah said to his brothers, "*I'll be back!*"

Let's get back to Dave's story; in two weeks Dave had no house and no income. Can you imagine his haters having a party? But little did they know that right after the fire Dave was coming back bigger and better. I speak into your spirit right now that right after the fire God is going to take you higher. For months Dave found himself in a helpless state. The banks were breathing down his neck for overdue loan payments and he was both homeless and unemployed. I met Dave a year later, underpaid and living with his in-laws, yet his faith in God was remarkable. He boasts with confidence, "By the grace of God, *I'll be back!*" You ought to shout out loud right about now, "Devil, *I'll be back!*

Some may ask the question, where was God in Dave's situation? I believe that God was the eye of Dave's hurricane, making sure that it did its job. God refines those He will bless, anoint, and appoint before He releases to them that which He has determined from the foundation of the world. While God does not take pleasure in our suffering (pain, agony, affliction), He knows that it is the suffering that releases the glory. Here's what the apostle Paul said in Romans 8:18: "I consider that our present sufferings are not worth comparing with the glory that will be revealed in us" (NIV). It is God's will that the things we experience advance, elevate and promote us in the kingdom.

Here's how God uses the devil: when He is ready to promote us, He sends the package with the enemy—the type of package the enemy would joyfully deliver to us; you know, trials and tribulations. But what the enemy does not know is that our next level is hidden within the package. Joseph told his brothers in Genesis 50:20, "But as for you, ye thought evil against me; but God meant it unto good." Likewise Jephthah's brothers meant evil against him when they thrust him out, but God needed him in Tob at the college of hard-knocks for preparation for the promise.

In my book *Lord Why?* chapter 3, "Lord, Why the Rejection?" we discovered that rejection is really divine direction. Some of the things you thought should not have happened actually had to happen so that God can get you to your destiny. I can imagine God looking at Jephthah's brothers and saying, "Right after graduation I will bring him back and promote him in your face." Wow, this revelation is sweet!

Let's get back to Dave. Dave was stripped to the point where he was totally depending upon God. Like Job in the Old Testament literature, God took his material worth, leaving him with his life. Dave was being set back for a greater comeback. John Christian Bovee once said, "A failure establishes only this, that our determination to succeed was not strong enough."[1] Dave was determined; Jephthah was determined. My friend, is your determination strong enough to succeed?

A few years later I saw Dave in the food store, and as usual I asked, "How is it going?" He said to me, "Anything better than I have now, God must have kept it in heaven for Himself." He said, "God has rebuilt, restored, replenished, increased, and enlarged me, right *in the face* (presence) of my enemies." Dave received more than he ever had; he was being tried (tested) in order to be blessed. This test of security made Dave a stronger Christian and allowed him to deepen his faith in God's ability to restore and increase. Dave was once again in a seat of prominence. Maybe the blows of life are tearing you apart. Ask yourself this question: Am I willing to trust God? Both Dave and Jephthah went down for a deeper foundation but in God's time were brought back up for the greater. *I'll be back!*

DELAYED FOR MATURING

The Word of God is indeed a weapon in the hands of those who would study it and apply it and it is truly the wisdom of God. James 1:2–4 for instance, tells us how to conduct ourselves in times of great trials. The writer says, "My brethren, count it all joy when ye fall into divers temptations; Knowing this, that the trying of your faith worketh patience. But let patience have her perfect work, that ye may be perfect and entire, wanting nothing."

Tests and trials are for the maturing of your faith, not to destroy, as many would have you to believe. The things that you are going through are a part of the Master's plan to get you to a level of complete surrender and trust in a God who said, "I will never leave you nor forsake you" (NKJV). Our faith must be tried as gold is tried in the fire, so that we can be purified from all impurities (1 Pet. 1:7). Faith that has not been tested is shaky and is not guaranteed to stand the test of time.

When an individual like Jephthah gets up to testify that God is a burden bearer or a Deliverer, he does so with conviction and persuasion because he can personally lay claim to such deliverance. Moreover, a threat to the continuity of his life and his destiny does not rattle him as it would the ordinary person since he is confident that God will work everything out in due season. In the diagram below I have attempted to illustrate just a few of the many aspects of spiritual growth:

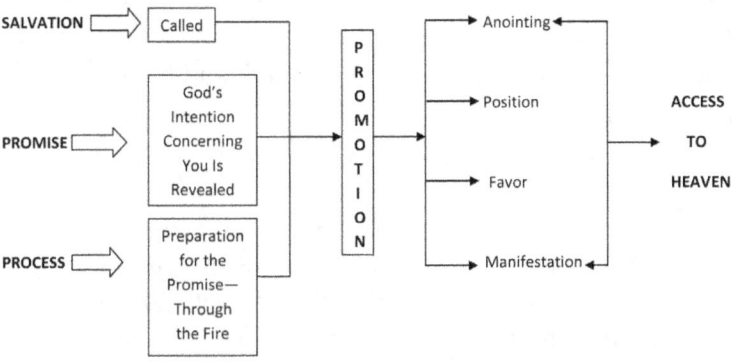

Notice on the diagram that the salvation experience takes place first, and then come God's promises concerning you, which is followed by a process (a time of testing), and thereafter comes divine promotion.

The writer of James reminds us that we will face various

trials; in others words, you and I will be processed. There are several underlying inferences that can be made from this statement. Firstly, trials are inevitable, they will come. Too often we allow the delays in life to frustrate us as we erroneously interpret delay as final. Someone once said that God has three responses to our prayers: yes, no, or wait. It has been proven that Christians often confuse the two latter responses—no and wait. While *wait* can feel like a *no* because there is little or no (or very little) immediate progression being made in our favor, God's *wait* may result in a futuristic *yes*. Don't let haste cause you to lose the blessings that God has ordained for you. Remember that God is a God of timing. Oftentimes if God gives us an immediate *yes*, we would mess things up because we are not matured enough to handle the weight of glory. *Delayed for maturing!*

Jephthah had to be prepared in the land of Tob before he could return back to his destined place to be promoted and eventually defeat the children of Ammon. I truly believe that God has delayed some stuff in our lives so that He can mature us to handle the mega, which, if received prematurely, we will lose it; and God will not allow this. My friend, you are being delayed to get paid, and God pays well. *In your face!*

The apostle Paul said to the Corinthians:

> And I, brethren, could not speak unto you as unto spiritual, but as unto carnal, even as unto babes in Christ. I have fed you with milk, and not with meat: for hitherto ye were not able to bear it, neither yet now are ye able. For ye are yet carnal: for whereas there is among you envying, and strife, and divisions, are ye not carnal, and walk as men? For while one saith, I am of Paul; and another, I am of Apollos; are ye not carnal?
>
> —1 Corinthians 3:1–4

Here we find Paul reminding the Corinthians that they were not matured enough to eat solid food (meat); hence, he had to continue feeding them with milk until such time of maturity. Too many people made bad choices because they felt as if time was running out on them or God was taking too long to move on their behalf. There are some things we feel we are ready to handle but God knows better. It is better to obey and wait it out than to rush into situations, only to have regrets later.

We had a saying when I was a boy: you rush the brush you spill the paint. God's choice, yes you. The picture God is painting for your life is too beautiful, and He will not let you spoil it. Don't rush the brush; it's just about that time and your haters will be invited to witness the revelation, elevation, and manifestation of that which God has purposed for your life. And guess what? He's going to do it right in their face! God could have easily made Jephthah captain over his brothers; but without maturing him, He knew Jephthah would have failed. God knows just what it takes to mature you and He will not put more on you than you are able to bear. Hence, wherever you find yourself and whatever situations you might be in, God has it under control. You are coming out victorious; it's just a matter of time!

Abraham Lincoln once said, "Give me six hours to chop down a tree and I will spend the first four sharpening the axe."[2] My comrades, God is sharpening you for the future and you've only been delayed for maturing; but you will be back and better than before.

Spiritual Giants Never Quit

Although a little confusing as to who Marvin Sapp refers to in his song, "Never Would Have Made it," the lyrics ring clear that the composer is familiar with maturing through trials, as he expresses in the song and I quote in part:

> Never would have made it
> Never could have made it without You
> I would have lost it all
> But now I see how You were there for me...
>
> And I can say
> Never would have made it
> Never could have made it
> Without You...
>
> I am stronger, I am wiser
> I am better, much better...
> I made it
> Through my storm and my test
> Because you were there
> To carry me thru my mess...
>
> I would have lost my mind
> I would have gave up
> But You were right there...

As Sapp alludes to in this song, the tests that you've faced last season should have made you stronger, wiser, and better. Yes, at times you may feel like you won't make it; but when God brings you out, you will look back over your past experience and sing for joy.

It is so easy to quit, but it takes more strength to continue in a battle that seems rigged (arranged, engineered) in favor of the opponent. Yet we know that on this Christian journey we must fight till the end; and even after we have taken the last blow, we must stand our ground, anticipating the champion of our soul (Jesus Christ) to step in the ring. Jephthah must have been extremely hurt, being called the son of a harlot, denied the rights to his inheritance, and then thrust out by his own brothers, who most likely he helped to raise up. He probably had to give the boys a bath, dress them, feed them, teach them, protect them, and even give of his own substance to them (Judg. 11:1–2). This may sound familiar to you—I know it does to me—after you would have done all you can to help folks they still turn around and bite (attack) you.

Elbert Hubbard once said, and I quote, "God will not look you over for medals, degrees or diplomas, but for scars."[3] Those with the scars that are still worshipping and giving God His glory in spite of the fiery darts are the ones God is going to display in the enemy's face. David said in Psalm 35:12, "They rewarded me evil for good to the spoiling of my soul." In other words, David was saying, I did them good but they still rewarded me evil. Solomon, David's son, came back saying God's got their number. The Bible declares in Proverbs 17:13, "Whoso rewardeth evil for good, evil shall not depart from his house." They are going to reap what they have sown (Gal. 6:7), and God will prove (establish, demonstrate) to your enemies that whom He blesses can no man curse (Prov. 3:33). *In their face*, God will spread you a table!

Spiritual giants never quit; we always come back better than before. I have been in great battles, storms, and hurricanes. I remember some years back when money was flourishing, my business was booming, and the finery of life was at my fingertips. And then time and destiny surrounded me, demanding I give God a yes; and yes, I did say yes. As a babe in Christ and with a burning passion to know God in His fullness, I decided to completely surrender to God, not knowing the depth of the Scripture that said, "Behold, I have refined thee, but not with silver; I have chosen thee in the furnace of affliction" (Isa. 48:10).

Well, one day I received an awesome prophetic word that God had brought me to the kingdom for such a time as this and that He will anoint me with an unusual anointing and I will travel around the world preaching and teaching the gospel of Jesus Christ and that wealth would come to me from the east, west, north, and south. I worshiped, praised, jumped, and shouted, not knowing that there would be a process before the promise. God will make you a giant in the spirit before He seals the deal (give you what He has for you). In my new book *Paying the Price*, I talked a lot about God's orchestrated mentoring fire that has been designed to prepare us for the promise. (You've got to get a copy of this book; it will help you understand the prerequisites [requirements] for the promise.)

In one day the courts came in and I lost everything I had; it was a *Job* experience for me. In the midst of losing my business, money, houses, boats, friends, and so forth, and not receiving the immediate one hundredfold promise of God, the temptation to quit appeared. But thanks to God, who kept me in the fight; and not only did He keep me, but has turned my pain into power and my shame into fame. God, in His wisdom, was allowing these tests and trials that I suffered to develop my spiritual muscles. The things that you have suffered and are suffering are only to develop your spiritual muscles so that you can handle the weight of glory that God has set aside for you. My comrades, *spiritual giants never quit!*

Jesus declared in Matthew 19:29, "And everyone who has left houses or brothers or sisters or father or mother or wife or children or fields for my sake will receive a hundred times as much and will inherit eternal life" (NIV). In turning our backs, as it were on family, friends, houses, riches, popularity, and fame, etc., we are free to cling to God. Too often these material things weigh us down and blind us from the perfect will of God.

The average human being is blessed with two hands, which are best utilized for gripping or holding things. In most cases, the more things we are required to hold or grip, the less space is available in our hands, thus, leaving little or no room to embrace another object. Hence, if we desire to embrace more objects, we must first release what is in our hands. This is why Jesus proposed that His followers be willing to let go of some stuff (the lesser) so that they can grab a hold of the greater. People who knew my past successes would constantly ask, "How did you survive when you lost everything?" My response was that God had a plan and purpose for my life, so He kept me. Yes, He stripped me of material gain; but at the same time He was using the pain to develop a spiritual giant. My friend, by the time God is through with you, your pain will become power. *In your face!*

The key to survival is to never quit, don't give up, and never call retreat. Experience has taught me that we must stay in the fight; because no matter how bad things may look, it's not over yet—the King still has a plan. For even when you have been knocked down and left to die, when persons would have made preparations to bury you, God still has the power to raise up dead things. Today may be filled with discouragement and misfortune, but tomorrow God can wipe away every tear. I am a witness, and I believe if God brought you to it, He will bring you through it. *Spiritual giants never quit!*

Calling Forth the Warrior Inside of You

There are more guts on the inside of you than you give yourself credit for. That which you need has already been given to you by God; all you must do is show up for the fight. The story is told of a community of giants who had created a village customized for their extraordinary height and grand size—everything was supersized, even their homes. However, one of the couples gave birth to a normal sized baby (which in comparison to the giants appeared to be a dwarf), who they named John. As John grew to be a man, he became more and more depressed because he was shorter and smaller than everyone else. Subsequently his friends would call him names and make jokes about his physical appearance. John felt like an outcast and insignificant. His parents could not console him. One day the neighbor's house collapsed and their baby was stuck under a pile of rubble. One by one the giants tried to creep under the debris but failed. Finally, John came and went into a small opening and brought the baby to safety. The villagers applauded John and that day everyone realized, including John, that despite his makeup he had the power to do great exploits.

Like John and Jephthah, you may feel unqualified and rejected, because according to society, you're not able. Despite your makeup or what others may think of you, God has designed you perfectly for the task that He has assigned you. While people may have counted you out and disqualified you, God has deposited in you the ingredients necessary to get you to the top. In all honesty, you may not feel like you are ready or perhaps it seems impossible, given your current situation. Just be assured that God equips those He calls—*calling forth the warrior inside of you!* Of course, when we are facing the opponent, it is easy to feel inadequate, especially if we have not experienced God in any profound way. So these tests and trials that you are experiencing serve merely to increase your faith. They will give you the stamina to fight the giants of disappointments, attacks from the enemy, abandonment, lack, etc. These are all training tools. At the end of the day, you will discover that the fight is rigged in your favor. Hence, we need not fear the adversary for God is on our side.

Satan wins every time we cry retreat, so he intensifies the trials and accelerates the attacks to make us shake and surrender in fear. The Bible says, "The devil, as a roaring lion…"

(1 Pet. 5:8). The key word in this passage of scripture is "as," which frees us from fear. Used in this manner, *as* infers that the devil is *not* a lion, but *as* a lion. In other words, there are some similarities between the devil and a lion, particularly his roar (makes a lot of noise), which can be confusing; but they are not the same. For instance, a lion roars with power and has the ability to destroy anyone or anything that enters his territory. However, the devil roars and makes a lot of noise to birth fear in anyone that is in pursuit of God and their destiny. While the lion may be king of the jungle and can back up his roar, the devil is king of nothing and can't do anything; God is in control!

Satan has no right to touch a child of God; however, God does use him and his cohorts (buddies, partners, allies)—you know who they are; those same family members, so-called friends, bosses, co-workers, next door neighbors, and so-called "anointed for this hour" church folks—when He is ready to promote you. You have been given authority to tear down Satan's kingdom and to expand the Kingdom of God. That's what the enemy is afraid of and he will use anyone and anything he can to stop you. Therefore, God is calling forth the warrior that's inside of you, the "you" that will not take no for an answer. *I'll be back!*

God allows opposition to come our way not to destroy us, but to bring out what's on the inside of us. Here's what the Bible says concerning the Israelites in Exodus 1:12, "But the more they [the Egyptians] afflicted them [the people of God], the more they multiplied and grew." My brothers and sisters, no pain no gain. It is out of pain that a woman gives birth to a child in the natural realm; and if she is bearing twins, triplets or more, you can only imagine the intensity of the pain. So likewise, in the spiritual realm a man or woman gives birth to their destiny out of pain and according to their assignment and the level of anointing, blessings, and favor that has been ordained for their life; the pain is rapid and very intense. The Bible declares in Micah 4:10, "Be in pain, and labour to bring forth." The more pain (trials and tribulations), the more you must push. There is a "you" on the inside of you that the devil doesn't want to surface.

Jephthah had to fight through the opposition of his own brothers. People will speak negatively over your life; but the blessings of God cannot be reversed by human curse (negative words). When people look at you, they may say that you don't have any significant point of reference; you are just a bunch of trash, a nobody. But God specializes in taking nobodies (insignificant people) and making them somebodies (significant). Remember also that God specializes in transforming trash into treasure. Jephthah is a prime example. He didn't have family clout, for his mother's status as a harlot and his illegitimate birth took such privileges away. According to society, Jephthah was a nobody; yet God took this young man and placed His stamp of approval upon him, giving him an inheritance among His legal sons and daughters, a heavenly status, and made him who once was despised, a hero in the face of his enemies. *In your face!*

I am sure many are asking the following questions: Why did God choose to work against the odds? Why did He not choose a man that everybody loved to lead the people? As is often the case, I believe if God had chosen another, he or she would have wanted to claim God's glory and forget who the praise belongs to. But when we are helpless, frail, and rejected, we are more prone to realize that our accomplishments are because of the grace of God. Jephthah knew his victory was only because the Spirit of God had empowered him and that his leadership was because of the favor of God resting upon his life. Hence, Jephthah approached every task with God at the forefront of his agenda.

Warren Wiersbe once said, "No person should be blamed

for the circumstances surrounding his or her birth. Why permit the things you cannot control to burden your life? Learn to accept them, and the Lord will work out His purpose in His own time."[4] Gilead's (Jephthah's father) wife bared him several sons; but Jephthah, the son of the harlot, was hated by her sons. When the boys were all young, they loved each other. But as soon as they grew up and it was time to share the inheritance of the father, then here comes jealousy, envy, hatred, division, and the "all for me" syndrome. No matter how many persons are fighting for your position, God will not let them have it. Gilead's sons felt that they should have been the only ones blessed and they were certainly the only ones qualified to be God's chosen vessels. Jephthah in the natural realm may have been birthed from the womb of a harlot, but in the realms of the spirit he was birthed from the womb of God with a specific assignment and an unusual anointing. Never let what you see determine who you will be. God is *calling forth the warrior in you!*

There is an anointing stored deep in the womb of your spirit that will activate the glory of God here on earth. When the Old Testament scholars researched the life of Jeremiah, it was discovered that Jeremiah's anointing was not bestowed upon him by human hands or the smearing of olive oil on his forehead; rather, Jeremiah was chosen and ordained before he was formed in his mothers' womb. The calling and favor of God on his life was not contingent on or determined by how successful or how brilliant a man Jeremiah grew to be; but the supernatural innate ability was given to him by God, long before the natural birth occurred. Like Jephthah, God has placed a calling upon your life that has nothing to do with your physical abilities. In fact, the anointing that you house will override all the failures of this natural realm and God will display you right in the face of your enemies. *I'll be back!*

The Word of God declares that greater is He that is in me than he that is in the world (1 John 4:4). Satan and his cohorts are no match for the Spirit of God that dwells within you. Hence, you need to walk in the confidence of a valiant (brave, courageous) soldier. It is so sad that Christians are living such defeated lives when God has given us the victory. Too often we, as Christians, buy into the lie that this is as good as it gets, when God has made us the head and not the tail. He has placed us above and not beneath; therefore, we need not settle. If we were on the front line by ourselves or perhaps fighting this battle in our own strength, then I would say run as fast and as far as you can! Yet God is working in and through you to accomplish His great plan in the earth; so it's very imperative for you to stay grounded. The God that we serve is greater than any enemy that will ever come against us. *Warriors come forth!*

One of my favorite hymns, "Jesus Hath Died and Hath Risen Again," attests to Jesus' ability to save His people. An anonymous writer states in the third stanza of this hymn, "Jesus is stronger than Satan and sin, Satan to Jesus must bow; Therefore I triumph without and within: Jesus saves me now." There is no doubt by the words of this hymn that Satan is no match for God. According to this hymn, it is not that we are so strong or powerful but it's because the Christ in us is all powerful. In other words, we have been endowed with power from on high and God is calling forth the warriors to use their endowment (abilities). *Use it or lose it!*

Jephthah experienced the finishing power of God, and so will you. Yes, the battle maybe raging and there is a real war going on. But, my friend, you have one of two options: either fight or flight. Fight for your future or die in your present. Jephthah had to weigh the attacks he was facing versus the future he was chasing. *In your face!* Yes, Jephthah was a warrior on the run. My friend, are you a warrior on the run; great, mighty, and anointed but still on the run? May I suggest to you that God is preparing you and when the process is completed He will bring you back for the promise. *I'll be back!*

While the Christians are sleeping, the enemy is wide awake, alert, and ready for action! The victory will not be won by sleeping giants nor will the prize be given to those that are not determined and willing to stay the course. However, victory is promised to us in spite of the oppositions. But we must exercise this confidence that God has placed the greater on the inside of us. There is a warrior on the inside of you that must come forth. *I'll be back!*

Prayer

Dear God, I thank You that Your Word is sharper than a twoedged sword (Heb. 4:12) and that it cuts and heals. Therefore, I send Your Word to overtake my future. Lord, I pray that during this temporary setback I will be of good courage, knowing that I will be back and that You will restore all that the locust and the canker worm has stolen from me (Joel 2:25). I pray, God, that Your perfect will be done in my life and what the enemy meant for evil has already been turned for my good (Gen. 50:20), in Jesus' name. Amen!

Declarations

I decree and declare that when God's time comes, I will be back to possess the promise, in Jesus' name!

I decree and declare that my delay has matured me for my pay, in Jesus' name!

I decree and declare that after the process, God will bring me back to possess the promise, in Jesus' name!

I decree and declare that I am a giant and I will never quit, no matter what comes my way, in Jesus' name!

I decree and declare that on the inside of me there is a warrior that God is bringing forth, in Jesus' name!

Chapter 3

A U-Turn

A Divine Shift

According to *The Free Dictionary*,

> A U-turn in driving refers to performing a 180 degree rotation to reverse the direction of travel. It is called a "U-turn" because the maneuver looks like the letter U. In some areas, the maneuver is illegal, while in others, it is treated as a more ordinary turn, merely extended. In still other areas, lanes are occasionally marked "U-turn permitted" or even "U-turn only."[1]

As it is in the natural, so it is in the spiritual. That is, God often finds it necessary to change the course of his children's lives to bring immediate success or to accelerate their faith. The path can appear to be familiar, one that is comfortable and/or prosperous, thus creating a false sense of security. Or it might be a rough, uncharted path filled with tears and sorrow. Whatever the case may be, in the fullness of time God intervenes and, as a vehicle on wheels, we are forced to make a U-turn to go in the direction that leads to the perfect will of God.

As *The Free Dictionary* notes, occasionally, on a divided highway, special U-turn ramps exist to allow traffic to make U-turns, though often their use is restricted to emergency and police vehicles only. This is also for the chosen men and women of God as they move forward; God at times will suddenly make an emergency shift and change their course. I know you are reflecting on the shifts that took place in your life; but I guarantee you that God's direction, though you may not understand it now, will take you right there to your destiny.

The Bible releases this knowledge in Hosea 6:3, "Then shall we know, if we follow on to know the LORD: his going forth is prepared as the morning; and he shall come unto us as the rain, as the latter and former rain unto the earth." In other words, what the prophet is saying is to trust God and to do everything in your power to become knowledgeable of who He really is, getting to know Him by reading about what He has done in the past. Read about how He took Joseph from the pit and brought him to the palace. Read of how He transitioned David from being a shepherd boy to reigning as king of Israel, and how He removed Vashti to make Esther the queen. My friend, when there's a U-turn in your life, remember that God is still in control. A divine shift can be painful, as it may move you from the known to the unknown, from friendship to rivalry, and from popularity to abandonment or vice versa.

In the religious arena when we talk about a shift, normally we use the term in reference to a change from bad to good. However, there are several references in Scripture that the reverse is true also, from good to bad. For example, the events surrounding the shift and the way the shifts were perceived by others were not always pleasant. In the story of Jephthah, we discovered that while in the process of a divine shift in his life he went from being a beloved brother to being rejected and despised by his siblings. For him the shift itself was painful; but God knew that it would yield an excellent return. Jephthah's position in his father's house resulted in his brothers despising him.

It is such a pity that we do not celebrate each other anymore. Do you know that there are people who will build their lives off of you and when you attempt to build your own life they will abandon you? Ask Jephthah, he built his brothers and in return they sought to break him down. However, as long as you can build them up, they are happy and will support you. Then when the tables are turned, these same people who you sacrificed for are nowhere to be found in your time of need. I am sure you have met some of those folks before; they have flattering tongues and empty promises. Some are bold and hang on to this line, "We are in this together and you've got to make it." If you are gullible you will easily fall for this line and end up with a broken spirit. But thank God for the shift; thank God for the U-turn.

One would think that promotion for Jephthah would be a plus for his family. Likewise, one would think that promotion for you would have also been a plus to those around you who knew that you have been through hardship. But it's not so; the spirit of envy (wanting what others have) is taking over families, friends, coworkers, and not to mention even the body of Christ. You would think the temptation to begrudge a brother or sister would be avoided once it is realized that their accomplishments benefit the entire family. Everyone wants to be the star; but there is only one Star in the kingdom and that's the King of kings and the Lord of lords, Jesus Christ Himself.

When Paul in his letters to the Corinthian church spoke about the gifts of the Spirit, he asserted that they were for the edifying of the church. The gifts that God entrust into your care are to build up the body of Christ not to bring glory to oneself. In the natural scope of things, we find that when a member of a family gets a job, the income goes to help the entire household. You might be saying he or she doesn't give me a dollar! True, but if that person is paying the electricity bill, phone bill, etc., all occupants in that house benefit from the supply.

Since Jephthah was the eldest child, I assumed he loved

and cared for his younger siblings and did everything he possibly could to benefit them. However, as they grew up his brothers' attitude changed towards him; and they could only see Jephthah as the son of a harlot, thus refusing him equal privileges and thrusting (forcing, pushing) him out. Nevertheless, in God's time, after Jephthah's preparation, God would cause Jephthah to make a U-turn, bringing him back to the place from whence he was thrust out, mishandled, and mistreated. He spread a table before him in the presence of his enemies, making him the captain, the man in charge.

God creates situations to bring to pass His ordained will. The Bible says in Judges 11:4, "And it came to pass in process of time, that the children of Ammon made war against Israel." God allowed the Ammonites to come up against Israel so that the same individual—Jephthah—whom they had thrust out, the one that God had favored, anointed, and appointed, would be their most wanted. God is getting ready to make the rejects the most wanted, and it's about to happen right in their face! A divine shift! What God has for you, it is for you!

Jephthah's identity was changing swiftly and those around him saw it. What an awesome God we serve, a God who can take a nobody like Jephthah and mark him with the seal of greatness. Here's what the Bible declares in Zephaniah 3:19, "Behold, at that time I will undo all that afflict thee: and I will save her that halteth, and gather her that was driven out; and I will get them praise and fame in every land where they have been put to shame." My friend, God takes delight in getting you fame in the same place you have been put to shame, get ready for A U-turn.

The shift came swiftly; one day Jephthah was rejected and the next day he was accepted. Judges 11:5, "And it was so, that when the children of Ammon made war against Israel, the elders of Gilead went to fetch Jephthah out of the land of Tob." We worry too much about the process, constantly crying, "God, I don't know how You are going to fix this." The truth is it is not for us to know how God will work it out. All we need to do is be confident in the God we serve, knowing that He is well able and that in His perfect time He *will* do it.

The Bible declares in Hebrews 10:35-36, "Cast not away therefore your confidence, which hath great recompense of reward, For ye have need of patience, that, after ye have done the will of God, ye might receive the promise." Stop looking at the present condition through the lens of doubt and impossibility and begin to trust God. We need to change the way we view God's ability to act in relationship to our situation. God specializes in impossibilities. My friend, you are being setup and the table is about to be prepared right in their face! *A U-turn!*

Being thrust out from his family may have been the most difficult thing Jephthah had to experience but it was a divine shift allowed by God to draw him out of that stagnated environment into the wilderness where he could receive ample training. How long does it take for a man to realize that God is searching for the outcast? There is a proverb that says, "One man's trash is another man's treasure." Gilead's sons grew up and threw Jephthah in the trash. They said to him, "You should not inherit in our father's house for thou art the son of a strange woman." These were his own brothers who refused to share their father's inheritance with him. In their opinion, Jephthah was not qualified for the inheritance. You will be surprised to know what people are willing to do to stop you from receiving the inheritance God has ordained for you. People will support you as long as you do not surpass them; but as soon as you begin to excel, jealousy is likely to occur. Well, they threw him in the trash but little did they know God was the trash collector (garbage man).

If God does not step into our comfort zone and allow

the water to be troubled (allow attacks), we would stay in those trenches that lead to death. Just as people can keep us tied down with vain promises, we can also place chains on our future because of insecurity and failure to trust God to move in faith. The Bible declares that Abraham staggered not at the promise of God instead he obeyed God and left his hometown to sojourn in a strange land, his faith in God was counted as righteousness (Rom. 4:20–22). (See also Genesis 12:1–4; Romans 4:17–19.)

Corrie ten Boom once said, "Faith is like radar that sees through the fog."[2] There is no time for staggering; we must believe God even when we can't trace Him, and in doing so we will watch as our enemies eat every negative word that they have spoken against us. Think about the times you have resolved in your mind to move from a dead end but because of the fear of trying something new, you stayed, enduring the unfruitful environment that was not inducing (instigating, activating) spiritual conception or birth.

I believe Jephthah was settled, but God had more in store for him. So God caused a happening to happen to get Jephthah out of that environment, knowing that after Jephthah's preparation He would bring about a divine shift in his life. This would cause Jephthah to make a U-turn back to the place of promise, to show His siblings that He (God) was in control, even from the beginning. Never desire to be around those that are familiar with you because your greatness can only be recognized in the midst of those prepared for you. God's promises are guaranteed. The best is yet to come. *A divine shift!*

God Is Turning It Around

We are living in a time when people would try to deny you your birthright. Once people can see that you have the potential to exceed their accomplishments, they will make it their goal to bring you down. I've heard of incidences where persons went to pastors, bosses, families, friends, enemies, and so forth, to see to it that they stop an individual from being blessed and promoted. People will go to the extremes to make sure that you do not elevate above them. Oh, but when God is for you, they might as well get their popcorn and drink, take their seats, and get ready for the movie. And guess what? You are starring and God is the producer. Your haters will have a nervous breakdown by the time God is through dressing you. And it's going to happen right in their face!

When we pull people down, we are actually fighting against the plans of God. We have to be careful not to interfere with God's agenda. The apostle Paul asks in Romans 11:34, "For who hath known the mind of the Lord? or who hath been his counsellor?" It is difficult to understand what God is doing in a person's life. There are times when the individual can't fathom (figure out) what God is doing in their own life. We become stumbling blocks in the pathway of God's people when we adopt the attitude that we can speak and act on behalf of God. There are precious jewels covered in rags, picking out of the trash cans and roaming our streets. Don't look down upon these folks because God can turn their lives around in a second. It is not up to us to determine who God will use. The choice is all God's, and His measuring rod is different from the ones we embrace.

It does not matter how long it takes for people to realize that God's hand is upon you; the time will come when they will have to openly confess that it had to have been God that has done this. Like Jephthah's brothers, many may feel you do not qualify to share in the inheritance. Through the blood of Jesus Christ, you are qualified. In fact, the Bible declares that we are joint heirs with Christ (Rom. 8:17). As an heir with Christ, we have the same rights and privileges.

If God then gave Jesus Christ all power in heaven and in earth, this authority lies within us also, as we abide in Christ. We find the Gospel writers making this very clear as they quoted Jesus telling the disciples, "All power [authority] is given unto me" (Matt. 28:18). Then later it is recorded that greater works will we do (John 14:12). God is ready now to make a shift in your life; He wants to bring you to a place of confidence and authority even as He did for Jephthah; so get ready for a U-turn!

The inheritance is yours if you want it. Many persons will try to stop you from receiving the inheritance God has ordained for you. The enemy will try by all means to deter you so that you can forfeit God's will for your life. However, the promises are for you and your generation if you will only trust the Lord to act on your behalf. God the Father has preserved your inheritance; and this shift that is so uncomfortable is just to bring you into it. The Bible says in Judges 11:6, "And they said unto Jephthah, Come, and be our captain, that we may fight with the children of Ammon." Yes this is the same Jephthah that they had despised and rejected; but God has a way of turning things around. Remember, this is how God gets His glory, in the turnaround.

I can guarantee you that whatever it is that you are experiencing will prepare you, propel you, and position you for the greater. There goes God's three P's for your future: prepare, propel, and position. Now, where are yours? Because He requires three P's from you as well—prayer, praise, and patience. With all that is within you, endure the discomfort, knowing that the end result is worth the rough ride. To prematurely settle because of the fiery darts will negate you of a full settlement (payment); so hang in there, God is about to turn it around. *A U-turn!*

Never fear or be weighed down because of the attacks of the enemy because your God is too powerful to be controlled, too mighty to be stopped, too wise to be figured out, and too faithful to fail. God has you covered, and whatever He has ordained for you cannot be taken from you. In fact, God will use these attacks for your good. God, in His wise providence, had ordained for Jephthah to be the chief, He just took him down a different road to get him to his destiny. Just relax; God knows just what road to use to take you to your destiny. And if there seems to be a dead end, like it was for Moses and the children of Israel at the Red Sea, don't panic; this is for the destruction of your enemies and the construction of your future. In other words, the fight stops here and now!

The Bible declares that they said to Jephthah, "Come, and be our captain" (Judg. 11:6). Wow, look at God! A U-turn! The devil is aware of the inheritance God has for you; so, often he tries to confuse your mind by stirring up trouble and confusion all around you If it's not in the home, then it's on the job; if it's not on the job, then it's in the church; if it's not your husband, then it's your wife; and if it's not your friends, then it's your enemies. The enemy will use any means and anyone to frustrate you to the point of walking away from your blessing. My friend, God is going to turn everything around for your good; He's just waiting until your enemies start celebrating. Then just as they become satisfied and begin gloating (rejoicing) as they proclaim you will never get the inheritance, you will never amount to anything, or you will never be the head; God will show up, turn things around, spread you a table, and bless you right in their face!

Don't let anybody deter (discourage) you in this season. This is the hour that God is getting ready to flood the earth with His glory. Divine favor is about to show up at your doorstep, even the more because your opposition has increased. God is just waiting on the right audience so He can show up and show off. A table is about to be spread in the presence of those that thrust you out and God is going to do it right in their face and all will know that you are the chosen of God. I am so excited for those who have been hated, rejected, ignored, pushed to the back, lied-on, misused, dumped, and even stamped; because God is getting ready to display you, for His Glory! Shout glory with me! *In your face!*

AN UNLIMITED GOD

The Israelites were famous for placing limits on God. Despite the miraculous signs and wonders they were privy to, they continued to grieve God. The psalmist writes:

> How often they provoked Him in the wilderness, And grieved Him in the desert! Yes, again and again they tempted God, And limited the Holy One of Israel. They did not remember His power: The day when He redeemed them from the enemy, When He worked His signs in Egypt, And His wonders in the field of Zoan.
> —Psalm 78:40–43, nkjv

Albert Barnes states, and I quote:

> And limited the Holy One of Israel—The idea is, that they set a limit to the power of God; they fancied or alleged [supposed]—(and this is a thing often done practically even by the professed people of God)—that there was a boundary in respect to power which he could not pass, or that there were things to be done which he had not the ability to perform.[3]

We must not provoke God by placing a limit on Him; God can create ex nihilo (out of nothing).

This dry season in your life is not by mistake. God is allowing it to prove to the enemy that no matter how low you get or what state you find yourself in, He has unlimited power and can at anytime finish what He has started in your life. Stop getting angry and frustrated over the past pitfalls in your life; these are excellent tools for God to elevate you. Therefore, don't become bitter when people oppose you; see it as an opportunity for God to groom you.

What was meant to make Jephthah bitter, God used it to make him better. To be bitter will force you into Satan's trap. The devil knows once you become bitter, it will influence your attitude and your actions and eventually cause you to forfeit the promises of God. God will allow you to be opposed so that in the fullness of time your greatness can be exposed. Take the limits off of God, He's sovereign. He can take you down and still bring you up; He can take you through it (the fire) and still bring you to it (the promise). My comrade, there are no limits in God.

Here's what the psalmist said in Psalm 66:12, "Thou hast caused men to ride over our heads; we went through fire and through water: but thou broughtest us out into a wealthy place." The psalmist was saying, "Lord, You allowed all these terrible things to happen to me. They beat me down; I went through the fire and through the water, but at the appointed time You brought me out of that situation and ushered me into a wealthy place, just to show how great You are."

I feel right about now we ought to sing, and I'm certain that Jephthah would love to join in:

> How great is our God—sing with me
> How great is our God—and all will see
> How great, how great is our God

At the end of the day they will all see how great is our God! God is using everything that you have experienced, are experiencing, and will experience to make, mold, and shape you for the future.

Look at the life of Joseph. God revealed to him in a dream that he would become great; but after sharing his dream with his brothers, he was thrown into a pit. From the pit he went to prison but ended up in the palace. Let go of animosity and take the limits off of God. He has a plan for your life; don't let the naysayers hinder you from moving to the next level in God. Remember that God isolates you before He elevates you! Get ready for a U-turn, because you serve an unlimited God!

When you are fully trained and equipped for the task, God will move you from the back to the front. Of course, promotion, whether spiritual or natural, always comes with opposition; but be steadfast and of good courage, you've got what it takes to make it to the top. Take the limits off of God! What looked like defeat for Jephthah was God in His wisdom preparing him for his kingdom position and assignment against the children of Ammon. God prepared this warrior, whom He would use to defeat the foe. God did not allow the Ammonites to come up against Israel until Jephthah was fully prepared (Judg. 11:4). Remember, God is infinite, all-wise, all-knowing and all-powerful. Take the limits off of God; He often takes you in the opposite direction to confuse your enemies. But when it's all said and done, they will know and see that God was taking you to your destiny. An unlimited God!

God creates situations for revelation. And when it's time, He will cause a divine shift to bring you in line with His perfect will. He will shift the heavens and the earth when it's time to move you in position. Jephthah was in an unfamiliar and uncomfortable place, the land of Tob; but when God's time came, the Bible declares, that the elders of Gilead went to fetch him (Judg. 11:5). When God's time has come, those who rejected you will have to seek you out for help; so take the limits off of God. He can do anything,

A U-TURN

anytime, anywhere, or anyhow; just be still and get ready for a U-turn because you serve an unlimited God!

PRAYER

Lord, I cry out to You and You promised that You will hear and deliver me out of all of my troubles (Ps. 34:17). I pray that as I pass through the waters, You will be with me; and when I go through the rivers, they shall not overflow me. When I walk through the fire, I shall not be burned, nor shall the flame scorch me. For You are the Lord my God (Isa. 43:2–3, NKJV). Thank You for my U-turn, in Jesus' name!

DECLARATIONS

I decree and declare that it's my time for a U-turn so that I can go back and get everything that God has promised me, in Jesus' name!

I decree and declare that this is my time for a divine shift, in Jesus' name!

I decree and declare that God is turning it around for me, right now, in Jesus' name!

I decree and declare that my God is an unlimited God and nothing will be impossible for me in this season, in Jesus' name!

I decree and declare that God is spreading a table before me right now in the face of my enemies, in Jesus' name!

CHAPTER 4

No More Stop Signs

The New York Department of Motor Vehicles *Driver's Manual* states the following meaning of a stop sign:

> Come to a full stop, yield the right-of-way to vehicles and pedestrians in or heading toward the intersection. Go when it is safe. You must come to a stop before the stop line, if there is one. If not, you must stop before you enter the crosswalk... If there is no stop line or crosswalk, you must stop before you enter the intersection, at the point nearest the intersection that gives you a view of traffic on the intersecting roadway.[1]

Persons who are in a hurry or late for an assignment often view these signs as a nuisance, but they can be actual life savers. Like the stop sign, a spiritual intermission (pause, rest) is necessary to allow us to focus on the will of God for our lives and is also vital to our survival as Christians. However, these are not to be viewed as permanent dwellings but merely transitional places.

The signs of the times are very clear, for this is indeed the season for the unstoppable ambassadors of God to come forth. The delays, denials, and sleepless nights will be replaced with divine favor. From where you are presently sitting, it may seem hopeless and dismal (depressing, dull) like this is the end. However, God has set aside a time when His children will be untouchable, unreachable, and incomparable. Like the gold that is set in the fire to be refined, once the impurities are removed and the gold purified, the refiner removes the gold and sets it to dazzle the eyes of the beholder. Once we would have undergone this season of purifying (testing and trials), there will be no more stop signs. God will set us in the presence of our enemies and before the multitude and allow His power, anointing, and favor to rest upon us. *No more stop signs!*

Oh, the joy of the Jeweler (God) who watches with pride as the onlookers marvel at His handiwork (His chosen vessel). Moreover, confidence and passion wells up in God's chosen as we ourselves become baffled at how God takes our discomfort and anxiety and turns them into a treasured memory. Once we have been in the hands of the great craftsmen (God) and have been exposed to His molding and refining process, there is absolutely no stopping us. For it is exactly as James declared: "My brethren, count it all joy when ye fall into divers temptations; Knowing this, that the trying of your faith worketh patience. But let patience have her perfect work, that ye may be perfect and entire, wanting nothing" (James 1:2-4). Rejoice, for that period of delaying, frustration, and pain is about to come to an end. Jephthah, after a season of delays, frustration and pain, finally came into his *wow* season, according to Judges 11:6, when the elders of Gilead came to beg his pardon and seek his greatness. God's apparatus (machinery)—yes you, after the process comes the promise; so get ready, there will be *no more stop signs!*

TAKE THE BRAKES OFF

According to *The Free Dictionary*, *a brake* is "a device for slowing or stopping motion, as of a vehicle."[2] Remember that God is in control of our lives; and if He's going to take us to our destiny, we must let go and let Him have His way. Take the brakes off! There is a song that Carrie Underwood sings entitled, "Jesus, Take the Wheel." Well, if He's driving we must let Him take the wheel, the accelerator, and the brakes. Could you imagine if I am driving you to a place that only I know of and you say to me, "Pastor Johnson, you take the wheel and the accelerator and I will handle the brakes"? Remember, I know where I am taking you having driven this road numerous of times; also I am aware of the potholes, dangerous curves, and the obstacles that are on this path. Therefore, I know when I can speed up or need to slow down, turn, and even when to press through some stuff.

Many of us cry out, "Lord, have Your way, do as You desire; where you lead me I will follow," but still press the brakes when things don't look good and the enemy is raging. If you are going to reach your destiny, you must trust God all the way. Even though you have given God control of your life and He has control of the steering wheel and the accelerator, if you are controlling the brakes, the steering wheel and the accelerator are still subject to the brakes. Therefore, if God wants to move you forward in His time and you panic because you are operating with your five senses, you can easily press the brakes and hinder the move of God in your own life. Stop pressing the brakes when God is pressing the accelerator to catapult you to an unheard of dimension in Him.

Some of us have not given the Master Planner (God) full control of our lives. We cannot operate by our physical senses (seeing, hearing, smelling, touching, tasting) and expect to experience the supernatural power, anointing, and favor of God. Here's what the apostle Paul said in 2 Corinthians 5:7, "For we walk by faith, not by sight." Paul is saying that in order to move into the glory realm, we must take the brakes off and walk blindfolded, not looking through the natural but the spiritual eyes, which are the eyes of God (His Spirit). Because truly only the Spirit of God can lead you to the unusual, uncommon, and incomprehensible presence, power, and will of God. Take the brakes off and let God usher you into greatness.

Too often we want to give up because of the rumors and character assassinations. We must endure the persecution; for while these vicious attacks can leave us wounded, we must quickly recover and continue in the press. As Jesus said to His disciples in Matthew 10:25, "If they have called the master of the house Beelzebub, how much more shall they call them of his household?" Let them bark, but just remember they can't bite because God has them on a leash.

I truly believe in my spirit that God is getting ready to bring some folks from the back to the front, from the tail to the head; and He's going to do it right in your enemy's face. They had Jephthah for the least but God exalted him, making him the chief in the presence of those who refused to give him what was rightfully his. The Word of God puts it this way, "Thou preparest a table before me in the presence of my enemies" (Ps. 23:5). Take the brakes off because there are *no more stop signs!*

We place too much effort in worrying about what other people think or how they will react. Yes, constructive criticism can be of much value and it is important to get regular feedback; however, when negative comments drive one to abandon their assignment then this can be harmful. Some persons make it their business to sow negative seeds and weeds of discouragement in our path so as to deter us from the mandate of God. It is during these times that we must take the brakes off, stand our ground, and remain steadfast knowing that the will of God shall prevail. Even if humanity exhausts every means possible to frustrate God's plans for your life, when the time is fully come, God's glory will radiate in and through you.

Just when they think it is over for you, God will show up and disappoint them. I believe Jephthah's brothers thought they had it made in the shade when they thrust him out. They celebrated under the impression that he was gone forever and his share of the inheritance would have gone to them. How senseless can your enemies be if they think that God cannot bring to pass what He said? Shame on them! It's going to happen, right in their face!

Jephthah was forced to leave his father's house, but little did his brothers know that his disappointment was because of his new appointment. God will push you out to bring you in. Take the brakes off and let God's wisdom move and shift you right into your destiny. There are some folks who expect you to fail and not to make it, hoping you would become a vagabond (beggar); but God will take you beyond human expectations. When God is finished processing you, you will be a force to be reckoned with.

Jephthah was forced to flee into the land of Tob where he roamed with a band of worthless men, just as David did when he was on the run from Saul; but they both made it to their destiny. And just in case you forgot, your God is a finisher. God often allows us during the process (time of refining) to be in the company of those that wants to assist but have no means to assist so that we do not become dependent upon human efforts but rather we lean and depend upon Him all the way. In addition, when we are left with minimum resources we begin to appreciate God's ability to make a way when there seems to be no way. Jephthah's exile in the wilderness was his highway to the glory. My friend, God knows what He is doing, so take the brakes off because there will be *no more stop signs!*

GOING BEYOND HUMAN EXPECTATIONS

The words of the psalmist became real for Jephthah, "The stone which the builders refused is become the head stone of the corner" (Ps. 118:22). He then goes on to say, "This is the LORD's doing; it is marvelous in our eyes," (v. 23). Isaiah expounds upon this as he exclaims, "They that wait upon the LORD shall renew their strength; they shall mount up with wings as eagles, they shall run, and not be weary; and they shall walk, and not faint" (Isa. 40:31). The same people that chased you away will one day realize that you have been anointed and appointed by God for their deliverance. Stay in position because when God is ready He will bring you back to that destined place, where He will anoint you in the presence of your enemies.

Here's what the Bible says after the elders of Gilead came to fetch Jephthah in Judges 11:7–8:

> And Jephthah said unto the elders of Gilead, Did not ye hate me, and expel me out of my father's house? and why are ye come unto me now when ye are in distress? And the elders of Gilead said unto Jephthah, Therefore we turn again to thee now, that thou mayest go with us, and fight against the children of Ammon, and be our head over all the inhabitants of Gilead.

Wow, look at the handiwork of God in operation as He turned what Jephthah's brothers meant for evil into good! My friend, just relax because God is taking you beyond human expectations. *In your face!*

When the elders of Gilead called Jephthah, he probably asked, "Why are you looking for me now? A few days ago I was the talk of the town, the child of a harlot; do you now want the child of a harlot to reign over you, be your captain, and lead you in a military battle?" Wow, who can stop God from being God and doing what He wants to do? It's those whom you least expect and whom the multitude reject that God is raising up in this hour. And remember, many are called but few has He chosen (Matt. 22:14).

Jephthah's heart was already broken; he had paid the

price for the anointing through the rejection of his own people. Now God was ready to display him for His glory. Here's what the Bible says in 1 Corinthians:

> Brothers, think of what you were when you were called. Not many of you were wise by human standards; not many were influential; not many were of noble birth. But God chose the foolish things of the world to shame the wise; God chose the weak things of the world to shame the strong. He chose the lowly things of this world and the despised things—and the things that are not—to nullify the things that are, so that no one may boast before him.
> —1 Corinthians 1:26–29, NIV

God took Jephthah beyond human expectations. His brothers and no doubt all those in the community thought that Jephthah was finished and that he had no future, but God had a plan that they knew not of and what they thought was rejection was actually direction. My friend, God has a plan for your life and what you're going through is to catapult you beyond human expectations.

Destined for Greatness

Even some of the greatest biblical characters were people of low esteem. Once I asked God, "How is it that every time You choose an individual You choose someone of low esteem, unqualified by human standards, or from a lowly background? For example, You choose Joseph the son of Jacob; Rahab the harlot; David the shepherd boy; Jephthah the son of a harlot; and many others." Then it became clear to me that God handpicks such persons so that He can demonstrate His wisdom, ability, and power; and at the end of the day, He alone will get the glory. He also knows that these persons would not attempt to steal His glory but they themselves would acknowledge that "God is a great God." In this season God is calling people that have been despised, rejected, and outcast to greatness. God is looking for the ordinary to do extra-ordinary things for Him. You are destined for greatness, and God is about to spread a table before you in the presence of your enemies. *In your face!*

Don't be alarmed when people say that you are not qualified. Remember, jealousy has no boundaries; but when God is through working on you, you're coming forth as pure gold. Remember, God can use any vessel He so chooses; and because you're destined for greatness the enemy is determined to stop you. Relax, there may be some speed bumps, potholes, and even puddles on your way to greatness; but God's got this, and you're about to experience the unheard of.

Walt Disney once said, "It's kind of fun to do the impossible."[3] You are about to shout when you see what God is about to do in the face of your enemies! Just what they said was impossible, God will make you familiar with. Keep at the forefront of your mind that it's not by power, nor by might but by God's spirit (Zech. 4:6) that He is going to accomplish His perfect will in your life; thus moving you from the back to the front, from the least to the greatest in the face of your enemies. You've been *destined for greatness*, and there will be no more stop signs.

Jephthah did not argue with his brothers when they expelled him from his hometown. Perhaps they wanted the inheritance for themselves and felt he was blocking them from receiving all, so they insisted that he leave. However, they did not understand what God intended for Jephthah could not be reversed by the plots and plans of man. Remember, we may not always like the strategies God uses to catapult us to our destiny, but we will love the results. God had a plan for Jephthah's life just as He has one for yours, you're *destined for greatness*.

It does not matter how people group up against you, just remain faithful, steadfast, and unmovable. Jephthah did not have to look for his job (kingdom position) after preparation in Tob, the job came looking for him (Judg. 11:4–6). The Bible declares in Proverbs 18:16, "A man's gift maketh room for him, and bringeth him before great men." Remember that God had predetermined for Jephthah to lead the Israelites during this time. Though thrust out, Jephthah had to be brought back for the fulfillment of the promise. The Bible releases this knowledge in Isaiah 55:11, "So is my word that goes out from my mouth: It will not return to me empty, but will accomplish what I desire and achieve the purpose for which I sent it" (NIV). My comrade, whatever God had promised you, in His time He will perform it.

Jephthah was brought back to the place where he was despised, bruised, and damaged so that the almighty God could spread a table before him in the presence of his enemies (Ps. 23:5). He became captain over the Israelites, including his brothers that thrust him out. Here's what the Bible says in Judges 11:11, "Then Jephthah went with the elders of Gilead, and the people made him head and captain over them." *In your face!* Watch the words of this text: "and the people made him head and captain." Wow! Is this text saying that God can make the same people who rejected you have to accept you and then turn around and bless you? *Yes, God can!* No more stop signs because it's your time for greatness!

If Jephthah had gone into the land of Tob and simply cried like a baby because of how they mistreated him, he would not have been ready for his God-ordained assignment. People cannot stop you, but you can stop yourself. Jephthah did not give up; he saw a purpose in his pain and pursued it through endurance. Many great leaders were forced to relinquish positions of prominence, later to embrace something of greater value. Winston Churchill, for example, was forced out of politics but later became the prime minister of Great Britain.[4] Don't despise humble beginnings (Zech. 4:10). God's ways are not our ways, neither our thoughts His thoughts (Isa. 55:8). Just stay the course and you will become the boss. *Destined for greatness!*

Prayer

Lord, I pray that I will humble myself under Your mighty hand so that You may exalt me in due season. I cast all my cares upon You for You careth for me (1 Pet. 5:6–7). I pray, O Lord, that I will hold fast the confession of my faith without wavering, for He who has promised is faithful (Heb. 10:23), in Jesus' name.

Declarations

I decree and declare that there will be no more stop signs in my life, in Jesus' name!

I decree and declare that I will take the brakes off and let God have complete control of everything in my life, in Jesus' name!

I decree and declare that I will exceed human expectations because I am God's choice, in Jesus' name!

I decree and declare that I am destined for greatness and great I will become, in Jesus' name!

I decree and declare that my God will finish what He has started in my life, in Jesus' name!

Chapter 5

Next Exit

Have you ever been driving or perhaps in a vehicle that has been on the highway for a long time when you slept and then woke, slept then woke, slept then woke again? Then suddenly—being frustrated, tired, and weary—you exclaim, "How much longer do we have left before we reach our destination?" Then to your surprise the driver says, "*The next exit!*" Too often people give up minutes before the breakthrough is scheduled to occur. God can turn around a situation that has been holding you captive for ten, twenty, or even fifty years in one day, one hour, one minute or even one second. Look at what Jesus did for the man at the pool of Bethesda according to John 5:1-9:

> After this there was a feast of the Jews; and Jesus went up to Jerusalem. Now there is at Jerusalem by the sheep market a pool, which is called in the Hebrew tongue Bethesda, having five porches. In these lay a great multitude of impotent folk, of blind, halt, withered, waiting for the moving of the water. For an angel went down at a certain season into the pool, and troubled the water: whosoever then first after the troubling of the water stepped in was made whole of whatsoever disease he had. And a certain man was there, which had an infirmity thirty and eight years. When Jesus saw him lie, and knew that he had been now a long time in that case, he saith unto him, Wilt thou be made whole? The impotent man answered him, Sir, I have no man, when the water is troubled, to

put me into the pool: but while I am coming, another steppeth down before me. Jesus saith unto him, Rise, take up thy bed, and walk. And immediately the man was made whole, and took up his bed, and walked: and on the same day was the Sabbath.

The Bible tells us of this desperate man who after thirty-eight years continued to seek healing despite his previous obstacles. Although the healing stream was in view, this man could not get delivered. He complained that when he arrived at the pool that there was no one to put him in and another would go in before him. He was overlooked, rejected, and mistreated; yet he remained hopeful. When Jesus showed up, the situation that caused this man thirty-eight years of agony disappeared instantly. Time is irrelevant to Jesus' ability to perform the miraculous in your life. This decade of stuff (bad experiences) can be history with one encounter with Jesus Christ. The next exit is your destiny.

The power to activate, delay, or deny your deliverance is within you. Don't get hung up on the situation or the time factor; God is well able. Like this impotent man, Jephthah was on a long road waiting for his change to come and then suddenly it came. Some of you have been on this journey for quite some time waiting on the manifestation of the promises of God for your life. And I truly believe the fact that you are reading this book right now it's your time. Turn on your signal light; the next exit is your destiny.

It is so sad how easily Christians give up; we have to fight. The Bible admonishes us that having done all, we must still stand (Eph. 6:13). Suppose this lame man had decided that after thirty years he was not going to wait at the pool any longer? Then he would have missed his breakthrough. To give up is to call defeat. As long as you are still in the race, your chances to win are much greater than the person standing on the sideline. We have to stay in the race regardless of how long it takes to reach the finish line. The crowd may not be cheering you on and the finish line might not even be in view; but if you stay in the race, you will eventually get to the prize.

It pays to wait on your change no matter how long it may take to come to pass. God has made you a promise, and perhaps it's been years ago and you feel like it would not come to pass. Hang in there; whatever He has promised He will perform. The Bible declares that God "is not slack concerning his promise" (2 Pet. 3:9), and, "God is not a man, that he should lie" (Num. 23:19). We can rest assured that God will come through for us despite the dark clouds and the obstacles that preface the blessings. Life can be filled with surprises. It may start out real rough, as if things will never get any better; but with God on your side, things can change instantly in your favor. It's like the old adage tells us that behind every dark cloud there is a silver lining. This place of darkness and despair is not the end; God will allow you to rejoice once again if you can only stay the course, for the next exit is marked success. *In your face!*

Get Rid of the Baggage

The Bible admonishes us in the Book of Hebrews to lay aside every weight: "Wherefore seeing we also are compassed about with so great a cloud of witnesses, let us lay aside every weight, and the sin which doth so easily beset us, and let us run with patience the race that is set before us" (Heb. 12:1).

In pursuing the things of God and apprehending that which God has for us, we must lay aside every weight (baggage). In track and field those competing wear light clothing, freeing them from excess weight that will hinder their speed in the race. In order for us to cross the finish line and receive the prize, we must get rid of the baggage. The word *baggage*, according to *Merriam-Webster*, is defined as "intangible things (as feelings, circumstances, or beliefs) that get in the way <emotional baggage>."[1]

What is some of the baggage (weight) that can prevent us from reaching our destiny? A list would include sin, anger, hurt, resentment, bitterness, unforgiveness, pride, arrogance, and, of course, people. The enemy knows that he cannot stop God, but if he can frustrate you and keep you stuck on past experiences you will never come into your *wow* season (the promises of God). These experiences—though terrible, nasty, bad, and painful—are the same tools that God uses to catapult us to our destiny. You must get rid of the weight, that heavy thing or things that is preventing you from soaring to the next dimension in God.

We all know that an airplane cannot take off when it is overweight with baggage (luggage). If it does, chances are that flight will never arrive to its destination. A few years ago an excellent pilot friend of mine, who usually flies me to the smaller islands here in the Bahamas, had a terrible crash and every person on the aircraft perished, over twelve persons. He was one of the best pilots I have ever flown with, but the cause of the crash is believed to have been overweight. Notice he was an excellent (skillful) pilot; but because of the overweight on the plane, the future of every person on that aircraft perished and not even his skills or know-how could have saved them.

My friend, baggage (weight) will take you down; you must get rid of the baggage. Jephthah had to release the pain of being rejected so that he could embrace the power and favor for which God was setting him up. The devil doesn't mind you taking off if you are overweight, because he knows you will eventually come back down. Like the apostle Paul, we must shake the devil off.

There is a story in the Book of Acts chapters 27 and 28

where Paul, along with many others, was drifting on the sea and had to swim to the nearest shore. They found themselves on the Island of Melita. Seeing they were weary, cold, and worn, the barbarous people on that island kindled a fire to warm them up. Paul gathered sticks to assist and placed them in the fire. Suddenly a viper (snake) came out of the heat and fastened on to Paul's hand (28:3). The Bible says that when the barbarous people saw the venomous beast hang on Paul's hand they were certain that he was going to die but instead Paul shook the beast off in the fire (vv. 4-6).

My comrade, here is the revelation: when you are experiencing the fire, (trials and tribulations) there is always a snake, a viper (anger, bitterness, unforgiveness, hatred, envy, and so forth) that will try to come up out of what you are going through and attach itself to you so it can weigh you down, poison, and eventually kill you. This is neither the time nor the season to carry baggage; you are too close to your destiny. If God is going to bless you in the face of your enemies, you must move out of His way. It's time to get rid of the load and allow the wind of God (His Spirit) to get in and under you and take you to heights and dimensions unheard of.

Remember, a plane cannot take off if it's overweight; and if it does, no matter how skillful and ready the pilot is, he and the passengers will not make it to their destiny. Jephthah could have easily allowed what he went through with his own brothers to kill his future, but he decided to shake it off and make the devil take it back. Get rid of the baggage so that you can take off, right in their face!

Here's what the prophet released in Isaiah 43:18-19: "Remember ye not the former things, neither consider the things of old. Behold I will do a new thing; now it shall spring forth; shall ye not know it? I will even make a way in the wilderness, and rivers in the desert." God wants to do something fresh, brand-new in your life; but you must forgive and forget. Forgive those who caused you great pain and suffering and forget the horrific past experiences that you have encountered. It's time to take off! The eagle-eye prophet Isaiah states in this text that God is about to do a new thing and now it shall spring forth.

There are two Greek words for *new* that I would like to introduce to you, one is *neos*, which means numerically new but yet still identical; and the other is *kainos*, which means qualitatively new (new in kind) but not identical. *Neos* means there are many alike, while *kainos*, which Isaiah is talking about in this text, means you have never seen the likeness before of what God is about to do. God was simply saying to the prophet Isaiah, "I will do a new thing with a new people that has never been done before. God is raising up, in this hour, a remnant of warriors that are totally different and carrying an unusual anointing (rare anointing), empowered with unusual favor, and doing supernatural things for the kingdom of God. Get rid of the baggage that you be not hindered because God wants to take you where no man has gone before. It's time to take off!

STAY IN YOUR LANE

As we run this spiritual race, we must remain focused at all times so that the enemy does not cause us to change lanes and miss out on the prize (the promise). The least little distraction can result in failure. When running a race in the natural, there are several rules of thumb to be victorious. Firstly, training and more training. Some folks are often deceived into believing that they are good enough and hence don't need to work out; but even the best of the best needs to train. A good runner knows that he cannot succeed in a race without previous training. Although training tends to be rigorous and very demanding, much like the trials that we face en route to operating in the fullness of God, yet without it failure is eminent. It is during the training sessions that our weaknesses are uncovered and we have the opportunity to improve.

The second rule is that the runner must wait for the prompt (usually gunshot) to begin running. If the runner goes before the prompt, he will have to return to the starting line and begin again. If a runner fails to run at the sound of the prompting because of anxiety or inattention, this can put him or her at a disadvantage in the race. Listening for the starter is very important and can only be done when one is calm and alert. There are numerous cases where saints have walked out on their blessings prematurely or because of procrastination and have forfeited the right to the inheritance. We must watch and pray so that we do not move too early or too late. The Bible says, "Be anxious for nothing but in everything by prayer and supplication, with thanksgiving, let your requests be made known to God" (Phil. 4:6, NKJV). There is timing in God, and we must be alert and ready to embrace our season when God's time comes. Jephthah had to wait on God's timing, Joseph had to wait on God's timing, and so do you.

A runner who is preoccupied looking at what his opponents are doing can't get far in the race. Hence, the third rule is to stay in your lane. Stop worrying about your neighbors' achievements or your co-workers' success. We waste too much time trying to be like others. In this season God wants to display people who are unique. There is no photocopy in God. He is not limited that He must duplicate; rather, we serve a God of creativity who is filled with adventure and vision. I know what your friends have or perhaps even your enemies have may dazzle your eyes, but you don't need to plagiarize (copy) anyone. Take the brakes off and watch God dress you with favor. And, by the way, your blessing is tailor-made and can fit only you. *Stay in your lane!*

Stay in your lane and don't watch anything! Like Jephthah, all that you need to be successful in this race is already inside of you. Don't cross over into someone else's lane and become disqualified. Too many folks are so busy watching others that they move right out of what God has ordained for them and into something that will eventually frustrate them. Make sure you're doing what God has empowered *you* to do. A bird in the air is a genius, a fish in the sea is brilliant, and you operating in what God has prepared for you will be mind-blowing. Stay in your lane, and like Jephthah you will see the salvation of the Lord. Stay in your lane and watch God elevate you in the presence of your enemies. *In your face!*

Pay Attention to the Signs

Signs are everywhere, some are easy to discern and others require more attention. On a road trip, for example, there are various road signs such as *exit, speed, slow, stop, yield, dead end, wrong way, one-way, U-turn*, etc., and even traffic lights. It is important while on this journey to greatness that you pay attention to the signs so that you would take the appropriate action. There are times when God will have you to take an *exit* from your environment (folks around you, familiarity). Or maybe because you have suddenly arrived at your destiny, it's time to take the next *exit*. He may have you *speed up* to accelerate you because there are no more *stop signs* ahead of you (hindrance). He may have you *slow down* so that He can mature you for where He is taking you. He may have you *stop* so that you will not move out of His timing. He may have you *yield* (give way) so that your opponents are free to do what they desire and destroy themselves. He also lets us know when we are heading down a *dead end* and wasting time with people or in places that are not significant to our future. He lets us know that we are going the *wrong way* or down a *one-way* and it's time to make a *U-turn*. Pay attention to the signs!

Traffic lights, for example, are a device used to signal motorists when to move forward, slow down, stop, or turn, etc., to control the flow of traffic. On a busy intersection these lights prove to be very beneficial, preventing accidents, confusion, and other misdemeanors. In a metropolitan community when the traffic lights are off, traffic becomes backed up for miles and accidents are more prevalent. Too often, without the aid of mechanical devices or traffic officers, people refuse to pay attention to the signs and end up in a crisis. It is so important that attention be given to signs whether you are joy riding, cruising, or racing!

Like Jephthah and many others, we find ourselves on a journey to greatness with many interruptions and abrupt detours. As you cruise along the highway heading towards the things that God has promised you, there will be signs and signaling devices that are strategically positioned at various intersections of your life to keep you on the right path to your destiny.

Your attitude during these times will determine the measure of joy or frustration you will have. In the natural when cruising on the highway, some folks arrive at a stop sign and wait patiently till it is their turn to go, perhaps singing a song or taking in the surrounding view. Another person arrives at the same stop sign and becomes agitated because they wanted to keep moving. Remember, patience is power. Robert H. Schuller once said, "God's delays are not God's denials."[2] These agitated driver's huff and puff at the stop sign, thus ruining a perfectly relaxing ride. My fellow brethren, remember that these signs are there to aid you so that you can arrive safely to your destiny. God, at times, will allow certain situations to come into our lives that will slow us down or perhaps bring us to a standstill. Instead of becoming frustrated over the process, use these times to enjoy the view and glean from the lessons being taught. Pay attention to the signs!

In Judges 11:2-3 Jephthah's brothers changed the course of his life when they drove him away and forced him to take another route. Like Jephthah, many of you may have been forced to take another route. And deep within your heart you believe that the shift will cause you to fail; when, actually, God in His wisdom has shifted you for your future. Perhaps there are situations in your life that are causing much hurt, disappointment, and confusion. It is possible that these are signs that you need to pay attention to because it might just be time to exit. An exit sign doesn't mean that your life is over; it may really mean that your life has just begun. In other words, you have exited the past so that you can enter your future!

In some ways Jephthah's life was placed on hold (stop sign) by his brothers, for they intercepted what seemed to have been a quick route to his success by denying him his inheritance. Life would have been easier for Jephthah if he had been given his inheritance; but God did not allow it because the only way for Jephthah to develop a relationship with God was to be rejected by man. Like Jephthah, when there is a stop sign we must obey, trusting God that He knows the way. *Pay attention to the signs!*

Some signs are given more attention to by drivers than other signs; however, all signs are important and must be heeded to ensure road safety. The yield sign, for example, requires the driver to be extra witty as it alerts the driver to any upcoming dangers or road conditions that are not obvious until the driver approaches it. The yield sign reminds the driver of the importance of looking both ways, giving way to oncoming traffic, and stopping if necessary for approaching vehicles. Despite who arrives first at the yield sign, all drivers must correlate (show a relationship) these efforts.

There will be events in your life that will require you to *give way* to others, don't think it robbery to do so; just yield in humility, knowing that God will exalt you in due season. Jephthah was innocent, and by birth he was entitled to the inheritance; but his arrogant brothers were determined to enjoy what was rightfully his. Jephthah had to yield to his brothers' wishes to get rid of him. But remember, when God is in control all things work together for the good (Rom. 8:28).

Don't let the devices, plots, and schemes of your enemies discourage you, because God always disappoints them. Continue pursuing God and you will see how great your end will be. Jeremiah 29:11 says, "I alone know the plans I have for you, plans to bring you prosperity and not disaster, plans to bring about the future you hope for" (GNT). Remember that God's plans always stands! Stay focused, pay attention to the signs and get ready for undeniable favor. *In your face!*

As the apostle Paul declares, "If God be for us, who can be against us?" (Rom. 8:31). Jephthah came to an intersection when his brothers opposed him and had to make a decision as he sat waiting for the light to change from red to green. He saw the signs and they all indicated stop, yield, and wrong way. In other words they were saying to him that you are not going to receive the promise without a fight. But God was saying, "This is just a detour (long way around), and after the process I will have you make a U-turn and there will be no more stop signs so that you can get what's rightfully yours."

Somebody ought to praise God right about now, wow! You may have been denied promotions, possessions, monetary gifts, or even cheated out of relationships unfairly. Stay in your lane, respond intelligently, and keep your eyes on the signs; because the next sign you see may be your destiny (next exit)—*in your face!*

Prayer

Lord, I pray Your word over my life and give You glory as I recall that You are my rock, my fortress, and my deliverer, my God, my strength, my shield, my high tower, and the horn of my salvation; in You I will trust. I call upon You, Lord, who is worthy to be praised, so shall I be saved from my enemies, in Jesus' name (Ps. 18:2–3).

Declarations

I decree and declare that the next exit is my destiny, in Jesus' name!

I decree and declare that today I rid myself of all baggage that has hindered my progress, in Jesus' name!

I decree and declare that I will remain focused and stay in my lane, in Jesus' name!

I decree and declare that I will pay attention to the signs so that I will not miss my moment, in Jesus' name!

I decree and declare that when I arrive at my destiny, everything that God promised me will be there, in Jesus' name!

Chapter 6

In Your Face

It Had to Have Been God

Many runners are tempted to quit; some out of fear of failure, others because of physical discomfort. The Bible declares that the race is not to the swift nor the battle to the strong (Eccles. 9:11) but to the one who endures to the end. Perhaps along the track the naysayers are shouting words of discouragement as you stride along. Or perhaps the speed of the other runners is making you feel like throwing in the towel. Remember, a runner who quits will never experience the joy of victory, for in order to win a race the runner must endure to the end. We are in a spiritual race and our trainer is standing at the finish line cheering us on. Don't give up, because there is a prize that awaits you and God Himself is going to reward you right in the enemy's face.

If you can hold out and keep the faith during adversities, the onlookers will have no choice but to exclaim, "It had to have been God," when they see your latter end. While Jephthah was going through the criticism and rejection of his brothers, I can imagine the neighbors gossiping and maybe going as far as condemning him along with his brothers. But when God's time came for Jephthah, the same ones that cursed him had to turn around and bless him.

Here's what the prophet Balaam said to Balak king of Moab in Numbers 23:20 when he wanted to curse God's people: "Behold, I have received commandment to bless: and he hath blessed; and I cannot reverse it." Here's the good news: the bad news is not final because the bad news is not a reversal of what God promised but rather preparation for manifestation. Often the aches of life's struggles might seem too much to bear. In many cases when situations are unexplainable and irreconcilable (opposing), the world stands in awe and often exclaims, "Only God can bring them out!"

Frank A. Clark once said, "If you can find a path with no obstacles, it probably doesn't lead anywhere."[1] God wants the world to see and know that what they called trash He can make His treasure. Jephthah was considered trash to his brothers so they threw him out, but God collected their trash and made him His treasure. And not only did God make Jephthah His treasure, but He also placed him to reign over the ones that tried to ruin him. *In your face!*

Like Joseph, who was thrown in the pit and then sold into slavery, many persons might have given up on you. However, in the fullness of time when God snatches you out of the pit of hopelessness and ushers you into a wealthy place, the onlookers can only conclude that there has to be a greater power that's fighting your battles. Jephthah had a greater power fighting his battles, and therefore victory and destiny were inevitable (unavoidable, certain). God is planting the feet of the remnant on solid ground, making them unmovable, unshakable, and unpredictable; all you have to do is hang in there until He gets through.

Despite the acclamations that are received in honor of the faithfulness of God in our lives, suffering is not a welcomed event. No, suffering is not programmed in our makeup under the list of enjoyment; so we tend to avoid this as much as possible. Yet we can only know the power of God to deliver (finish what He has started), provide, and sustain us when we are opposed by the most furious predators that the enemy can use. My comrade, hang in there because the harder the push the bigger the promise. And the good news is that God is going to deliver your stuff right in their face.

There was very little or perhaps no joy in Jephthah's experience as he left the comfort of his father's home. It must have been very difficult. He found little or no pleasure in the interruptions of the normalcy of his life. He went from the protective environment of his home to hanging out with renegades. In a carnal spirit of discernment, many would be left with the question, 'How can God bring fame out of shame?' It is hard to see how God will use such bleak situations for His glory, while at the same time giving us a story (testimony). Remember, you and I can never control God and He will always take us down the road that He has paved to bring us to our destiny. And even though there may be a shorter route, most of the time He takes us the longer way so that He can mold and shape us for the part we have to play. Jephthah could have gotten the promise while at his father's house, but I can assure you that he would have lost it because he was not prepared for it. So God in His wisdom took him out from among his brethren unprepared and brought him back fully prepared and then gave him his overflow, right in their face! (Judg. 11:11).

God is going to do great things in the life of His children but not without pruning and removing the rough edges. The pruning is often not a pleasant feeling, but the rewards supersede the pain encountered during the process. While the one being pruned will experience great pain, it is guaranteed that they will come out with great power (divine favor). Therefore, as you go through hardship (e.g., pruning), be mindful that your God is in control of all things at all times and He knows how to bring you to the top even by way of the bottom. And at the end of the day, your enemies will say that it had to have been God that has done it for you. *In your face!*

The sweetness of the prize and priceless look on the enemy's face when he or she realizes that God has brought you from that (the past) to this (the future) is worth every tear dropped from your eyes. In the Old Testament's account of the life of Daniel in Daniel 6, for example, we find a true servant of God in the person of Daniel. Daniel was thrown in the lion's den, where his enemies thought would be his end. The next day they met Daniel relaxing in the den with his pet lions. Without blowing his own victory horn, the king confessed that Daniel's God was the God to serve (vv. 26–27). My friend, at the end of the day, your haters are going to realize that there is only one God and whom He blesses can no man curse. Daniel publicly stood for God by not bowing during his season of testing; therefore, God publicly blessed him in the presence of his enemies. *In your face!*

Just be reminded that the more the enemies, the larger the audience, and the larger the audience, the sweeter the victory. Like Jephthah, God is getting ready to bless you right in your enemies' face. The psalmist declares, "The Lord prepares a table before me in the presence of my enemies" (Ps. 23:5). Get ready, because God is preparing you a table in the presence of your enemies. When the den was opened and Daniel came out, the God of heaven caused Daniel's accusers to fall into their own ditch by allowing them to be thrown into the lion's den that they had thrown Daniel in (Dan. 6:23–24). And guess what? They did not have Daniel's God on their side. These events came about because of jealousy; the men were jealous of Daniel even as Jephthah's brothers were jealous of him. But you and I know that no man can stop what God has started. God's choice, yes you; disaster may want to kill you but destiny won't let you die. Just allow God to take top priority in your life and I guarantee you that no weapon formed against you will prosper (Isa. 54:17).

Perhaps your enemies are calling a meeting to plan your funeral or to celebrate your failure. Whatever the predicament you might find yourself in, God is able to bring you through it. While you are in the midst of a quandary (dilemma), it is difficult to digest these words; but trust me, if you can hold on and keep the faith, God will bring you through this. I've had some hard blows; some took me by surprise and others I saw coming but did not have the strength to get out of the way. In the midst of it all, I felt I would die and at times I wanted to die. It seems as if it would never end—one thing after the other. While weeping and wailing, I wondered if I would ever cross over this Jordan into my promise. In my heart, I kept hearing a still small voice saying, "Hang in there. Don't give up. Things will get better because I've got a plan in all of this.' Now looking back over those days I can truly say, "Hang in there, things will get better. God has a plan, and you will have the last laugh."

Yes my friend, God is preparing a grand entrance for you. And when the time is right, the banquet table will be smack dab in the middle of your enemy's face. Leave your enemies to God; God is preserving them for your day of elevation. The Bible declares in Isaiah 46:10, that God declares the end from the beginning. You may not see it at the moment, but God is about to bless you openly, right in the face of those who were hoping you would disappear. God is not going to enlarge your territory until your haters multiply. Let them say what they want and plan until they are tired; it is God who has the last word. They may be laughing at you now, but God will make sure that you have the last laugh. Hold on; don't give up; hang in there; because packaged, sealed, and delivered is the season you have just entered. This is where God has packaged what He has promised you, sealed it, and now its delivery time and that He will do, right in your enemies' face! *In your face!*

Prayer

I pray that in this crucial time of my life that You, Lord Jesus and my God and Father, who has loved me with an everlasting love and given me consolation and good hope by grace, will comfort my heart and establish me in every good word and work, in Jesus' name, Amen (2 Thess. 2: 16–17).

Declarations

I decree and declare that I am unstoppable because God is on my side, in Jesus' name!

I decree and declare that because of the faithfulness of my God, my enemies will see just what He said, in Jesus' name!

I decree and declare that my disappointments set me up for my new appointment, in Jesus' name!

I decree and declare that now I am empowered for the greater, in Jesus' name!

I decree and declare that in their face, God will bring to pass what He has promised me, in Jesus' name!

Notes

Chapter 1—A Temporary Setback

1. *The Free Dictionary*, s.v. "setback," http://www.thefree dictionary.com/setback (accessed October 16, 2014).
2. Tommy Lasorda, "Tommy Lasorda Quotes," *Goodreads Inc.*, http://www.goodreads.com/quotes/23953-the-difference-between -the-impossible-and-the-possible-lies-in (accessed October 16, 2014).
3. John Maxwell, *BrainyQuote*, http://www.brainyquote.com/ quotes/quotes/j/johncmaxw383606.html (accessed October 17, 2014).
4. William Shedd, "William G.T. Shedd Quotes," *Goodreads, Inc.*, http://www.goodreads.com/quotes/1388-a-ship-is-safe-in -harbor-but-that-s-not-what (accessed October 17, 2014).
5. Ralph Waldo Emerson, "Ralph Waldo Emerson Quotes," *Goodreads, Inc.*, http://www.goodreads.com/quotes/1204575-big-jobs -usually-go-to-the-men-who-prove-their (accessed October 17, 2014).
6. Booker T. Washington, "Booker T. Washington Quotes," *Goodreads, Inc.*, http://www.goodreads.com/author/quotes/84278 .Booker_T_Washington (accessed October 17, 2014).
7. Roger Banister, *BrainyQuote*, http://www.brainyquote.com /quotes/quotes/r/rogerbanni140368.html (accessed October 17, 2014).

Chapter 2—I'll Be Back

1. Christian Bovee, *BrainyQuote*, http://www.brainyquote.com/ quotes/quotes/c/christiann149448.html (accessed October 17, 2014).
2. Abraham Lincoln, *BrainyQuote*, http://www.brainyquote.com/ quotes/quotes/a/abrahamlin109275.html (accessed October 17, 2014).
3. Elbert Hubbard, *BrainyQuote*, http://www.brainyquote.com/ quotes/quotes/e/elberthubb384301.html (accessed October 17, 2014).
4. Warren Wiersbe, *With the Word Bible Commentary* (Nashville, TN: Thomas Nelson, 1993).

Chapter 3—A U-Turn

1. *The Free Dictionary*, s.v. "U-turn," http://encyclopedia.the freedictionary.com/U+Turn (accessed October 18, 2014).
2. Corrie ten Boom, "Corrie ten Boom Quotes," *Goodreads Inc.*, http://www.goodreads.com/quotes/264407-faith-is-like-radar -that-sees-through-the-fog--- (accessed October 18, 2014).

3. Albert Barnes, *Notes on the Old Testament: Psalms* (Grand Rapids, MI: Baker Book House, 1985), found at "Barnes' Notes on the Bible: Psalm 78:41," *Biblos.com*, http://bibleapps.com/commentaries/psalms/78-41.htm (accessed October 18, 2014).

Chapter 4—No More Stop Signs

1. New York State Department of Motor Vehicles, *Driver's Manual* (Albany, NY: DMV, 2013), 37-38, http://dmv.ny.gov/brochure/mv21.pdf (accessed October 19, 2014).
2. *The Free Dictionary*, s.v. "brake," http://www.thefreedictionary.com/brakes (accessed October 19, 2014).
3. Walt Disney, *BrainyQuote*, http://www.brainyquote.com/quotes/quotes/w/waltdisney100644.html (accessed October 19, 2014).
4. "Churchill, Winston," *International Encyclopedia of the Social Sciences,* 2008, *Encyclopedia.com*, http://www.encyclopedia.com/topic/Winston_Churchill.aspx#4 (accessed October 19, 2014).

Chapter 5—Next Exit

1. *Merriam-Webster OnLine*, s.v. "baggage," http://unabridged.merriam-webster.com/collegiate/baggage (accessed October 19, 2014).
2. Robert Schuller, *BrainyQuote*, http://www.brainyquote.com/quotes/quotes/r/roberthsc380574.html (accessed October 20, 2014).

Chapter 6—In Your Face

1. Frank Clark, *BrainyQuote*, http://www.brainyquote.com/quotes/quotes/f/frankacla156704.html (accessed October 20, 2014).

About the Author

Apostle Dr. Reno I. Johnson is a man guided by the Holy Spirit; he is an ambassador of Christ, he is a Warrior in the faith, an excellent Teacher of God's Word and a Dynamic, Radical Preacher. In addition, he is an author, who has written many books that have broaden the scope of individuals globally and they have helped to usher lost souls into the Kingdom of God. He is married to Shandaly Johnson and has one son and two daughters.

Apostle Johnson was ordained as a Minister at The Voice of Deliverance Disciple Center Ministries, Nassau Bahamas where he served for over thirteen years. By divine appointment today, the call and power of God is being demonstrated in the life of Apostle Johnson in such an awesome way. His unconditional love for people and passion for God's Word has been a transportation that has taken him throughout The World at large preaching the Good News of the Gospel of Jesus Christ.

Most notably, he is the president and Chief Executive Officer (CEO) of Reno I. Johnson Ministries International. He was consecrated to the Office of an Apostle on Sunday, December 5, 2010. He is also the founding pastor of Total Life Church, Orlando, Florida and Divine Encounter Ministries International in Nassau, The Bahamas.

Equally important, he has obtained an Associate Degree from New England Institute of Technology- West Palm Beach, Florida. However, upon receiving the call to ministry Apostle Johnson pursued several Biblical Degrees including a Diploma in Biblical Studies from Liberty

University (Lynchburg, Virginia), an Associate Degree in Biblical Studies, and also an Honorary Doctorate Degree in Theology from Bethel Christian University, At present, he is pursuing higher academia in Theology.

Apostle Johnson is a highly sought after anointed messenger of God, whose passion is to win souls for Christ, and advance the Kingdom of God. 'Touching people, Transforming lives'

Contact the Author

You can email the author at
renoijohnson@gmail.com or rijmintl@gmail.com

Please visit the author's website for current phone numbers and address.

www.arjm.org

To order any of Apostle Dr. Reno I. Johnson's Ministry Resources, Please visit our website, write or call us Today!

For Speaking Engagements please call or email us Today.

Connect with us on social media!

Don't forget to visit our Website!

Other Books by the Author

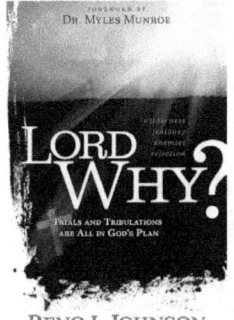

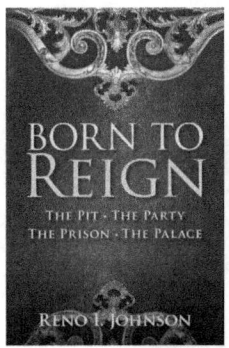

www.ingramcontent.com/pod-product-compliance
Lightning Source LLC
Chambersburg PA
CBHW050603300426
44112CB00013B/2053